Flight From Colditz

Would the Second World War's Most Audacious
Escape Plan Have Succeeded?

Flight From Colditz

Would the Second World War's Most Audacious
Escape Plan Have Succeeded?

Tony Hoskins

Foreword by Regina Thiede

Frontline Books

FLIGHT FROM COLDITZ
Would the Second World War's Most Audacious Escape Plan Have Succeeded?

This edition published in 2016 by Frontline Books,
an imprint of Pen & Sword Books Ltd,
47 Church Street, Barnsley, S. Yorkshire, S70 2AS

ISBN: 978-1-47384-854-2

CIP data records for this title are available from the British Library

For more information on our books, please visit
www.frontline-books.com,
email **info@frontline-books.com**
or write to us at the above address.

Printed and bound by CPI Group (UK) Ltd, Croydon, CR0 4YY [TBC]

Typeset in 10.5/13.25 point Palatino

Contents

Foreword

by Regina Thiede

In its 1,000 year history Colditz Castle has seen much change and its glamorous days as a royal dwelling now lie far in the past. In the early 16th century, Colditz was one of the favourite castles of the Elector of Saxony, Frederick the Wise. However, in the ensuing centuries, the huge architectural ensemble was put to more utilitarian use and it served variously as a workhouse, mental asylum, prison, PoW camp and hospital. In Eastern Germany the remains of the magnificent furnishings from the Renaissance vanished under practical hospital walls, as did the escape tunnels dug by the Allied prisoners of war who were detained here. German historians have tended to overlook Colditz Castle and very little research was undertaken until recently.

In 2003, when Colditz Castle was included in the group of state-owned Saxon palaces, castles and gardens ('Staatliche Schlösser, Burgen und Gärten Sachsen gGmbH'), it was in a ruinous state. Since then, about €20m have been invested to repair roofs, renovate facades, conserve ceiling paintings and preserve the escape tunnels.

The precious remnants of the Renaissance furnishings are in close proximity to the sites of famous escape attempts. The tunnel in the 'Dutch Buttress', for instance, crosses the last remaining Saxon garderobe pit (lavatory) of Frederick the Wise in Saxony. The wall of the 'Kirchenhaus', which the Allied prisoners had planned to break through in order to launch their glider, dates back to the fifteenth century and thus it was out of the question to destroy it for the glider project in 2012. In the process of restoration and rebuilding, the staff in the castle are constantly challenged with how best to preserve disparate elements from various periods.

SCHLÖSSERLAND SACHSEN
STAATLICHE SCHLÖSSER, BURGEN UND GÄRTEN

www.schloesserland-sachsen.de

In fact, the discussions have only just started. The 'Kirchenhaus' is the first building which has been fully restored; in the 'Kellerhaus' just the historical ceiling paintings have been preserved. The larger part of the castle is still waiting to be rediscovered and it is not yet open to the public. We hope to undertake further building projects in the next few years, including to restore the 'Kellerhaus' and the 'Fürstenhaus' to open a large new museum which will display all the periods and different uses of Colditz Castle. Many of the stories here could be told in the places where they actually happened as the whole castle is a lively institution integrating 600 years of building history and only a few things have been completely demolished. This means visitors will not find themselves in an old-fashioned exhibition where everything is in chronological order, but that they will be able to experience the varied web of history where it happened in an interesting and colourful way.

When I learned that the film team led by Tony Hoskins was going to come to Colditz in March 2012 to reconstruct and launch the famous glider, I was afraid that the entire project would be thwarted by the foul weather of an early German spring. Luckily things turned out differently. The project was blessed by a constant high pressure front and on 17 March the glider was launched into a crystal-clear sky. These were the craziest and most exciting fourteen days I ever had in my job at Colditz Castle, since the film team was as enthusiastic about the castle and its history as I am. They generated as much positive energy at this permanent construction site as I have ever experienced here. The media response was enormous and the number of visitors in the following summer literally exploded.

The present co-operation with the British and with all the other nations who are connected by the dark periods of the last century is a wonderful experience. It helps us in planning and constructing the museum and it inspires our work here at Colditz.

Regina Thiede
Curator, Colditz Castle
October 2015

Introduction

As our interest in the military machinery of the two world wars continues to thrive year on year and the generation who lived through the last world conflict for real slowly leave us, our only exposure to the ingenuity and sacrifices made by those men and women of the early 20th Century is in the books, the museums, and the factual documentaries made by those keen to tell their stories to a wider audience.

The technological advances made during the six bloody years of the Second World War were both considerable and rapid. Born entirely out of the need to defeat the opposing countries' armed forces, the progression of the war machine grew at such a rate that our understanding of engineering advanced comparatively decades ahead of where it been in the 1930s.

Whilst the cars of the day sported wire-spoke wheels, manual magneto advance and wooden chassis, the front line fighters built of the latest alloy materials flew hundreds of miles at speeds in excess of 300mph and regularly to heights previously only achieved on special record-breaking flights. The desire to deliver bigger, faster and heavier steel projectiles brought about bigger airframes, more powerful engines and increasingly sent the young generation of the time off across the skies, seas and lands of Europe.

Many of that time did not return home, the fortunate ones of those finding themselves in the prison camps of countries such as Germany and Poland. Here their resolve to fight did not wain and in line with the directives given in their training, they continued with their duties of escape and evasion.

My interest in this period has been with me since I was a little boy. For at least twenty-five years I have followed their actions, and consider myself fortunate to have been involved with a number of exciting ventures and projects in that time. Being asked to be a part of the Colditz glider project was an opportunity to not only bring the incredible achievement of those prisoners of war to a greater audience, but to also discover first hand some of the challenges faced by these men.

Tony Hoskins
Sussex, 2016

Acknowledgements

A great many people have been involved with this project from its early conception. Unfortunately, they are too numerous to all be named individually; most appear over the following pages. However, I owe a great many thanks for the success of what was achieved in the spring of 2012 in Germany to a lot more.

Firstly, I must thank my publishers, Martin Mace and John Grehan, who encouraged me in the first instance to write this book – without their enthusiasm I would never have begun typing. Also Mark Hillier, who I could rely on regularly to remind me that no matter how daunting, it would all come together well in the end! To everybody else not mentioned elsewhere, I have done my very best to include specific people or teams of people who have all played their part and I do hope I cause no offence if anybody or any group has been accidentally left out.

In no particular order, the following individuals or organisations have all been invaluable during the research and preparation for the Colditz project itself and many subsequently with the writing of this book: Pam Smith (née Goldfinch); Cathy Goddard; Mary and Maurice Flude; Andy Russell and Ian Woodfinden of the Colditz Society; David and Peter Underwood; Regina Thiede and all her staff at Colditz; Reinhard Schott; Bettina Bergstedt; Helmut Fendt; Steffi Schubert; Ralf Gorny; Andy Drabek and Frank Modaleck of the Flugwelt Altenburg Nobitz e.V; Colin Simpson, Paul Haliday, Gary Pullen, and Glyn Bradney of the Glider Heritage Centre Lasham; Andrew and Philip Panton of the Lincolnshire Aviation Heritage Centre; Ian Hancock and David Dawson of the Norfolk and Suffolk Aviation Museum; Martin

Francis; Steve and Joolz and the team at Audio Production Services; Robert Welford and team at Cambridge Gliding Club; Steve Codd, Richard Fitch, and all at the Surrey Hills Gliding Club; Robert Mitchell, for his work on the images; Hugh Hunt; Liz Weald of Channel 4; Ian Duncan and his entire team at Windfall Films; and finally my team at South East Aircraft Services for working hard to keep the regular work flowing alongside this project.

Where possible I have tried to gain copyright permission for all material contained within this book. If any credits have been missed or incorrectly stated then I will ensure that any future publications are corrected.

Part One

Chapter 1

Offizierslager IV-C
Colditz Castle

It made sense, it would seem, to place the most troublesome Allied prisoners in one place where they could be carefully watched and guarded. That place was the notorious *Schloss* Colditz deep in eastern Germany. What that decision meant in reality was that that Colditz was turned into a hotbed of industry and invention, with some thirty prisoners making successful escapes back to Allied or neutral territory. There were also countless failed attempts, some of which were quite brilliant in their conception. The most remarkable of these was the plan to build a glider and fly over the walls to freedom – the most ambitious and extraordinary escape story of all time. This is that story.

Flight Lieutenant L.J.E. 'Bill' Goldfinch was looking out of the window of Flying Officer Keith Milne's room. It was the winter of 1943-1944 and deep in the heart of Saxony it was snowing. As he stared out of the window he watched the snowflakes swirling upwards and over the roof of the castle – and it gave him an idea.

Keith Milne had been dreaming up escape schemes since being part of the first batch of British and Commonwealth prisoners taken into Colditz castle. The castle, in its current form, dates back to the early sixteenth century when it was rebuilt following a fire caused by its incumbent baker. Further restructuring had taken place in the nineteenth century when it was used primarily as a sanatorium for the wealthy. During the First World War *Schloss* Colditz became a hospital and when the Nazis came to power in the 1930s it became a political prison. With the need for a high security prisoner-of-war facility following the outbreak of war in 1939, *Schloss* Colditz became

Offizierslager, or *Oflag*, IV-C, for prisoners of officer rank only, with Polish servicemen as its first inmates.

These were followed in October 1940 by the first British and Commonwealth prisoners, which included Milne. Soon, Belgian, French and Dutch officers joined the growing number of prisoners which, by the end of July 1941, amounted to more than 500 men, almost half of whom were French. The British contingent at this stage was a mere fifty.

It was the only high-security prison of its kind in Germany, containing only officers and, where possible, their orderlies. Though the castle was built on an outcrop of rock, with a sheer drop of 250 yards down to the River Mulde, and the fact that Colditz was 400 miles from any frontier not under German control, the prisoners began escape planning from almost the day they first arrived – and they continued to do so throughout the months and years that followed, becoming ever more daring and ingenious.

A tunnel seemed at first to offer the greatest prospect of success and in January 1941 Captain Pat Reid took charge of the digging, but German suspicions were roused at an early stage and it was abandoned. The men, with nothing else to occupy their hands and minds other than escape, continued to examine every part of the building for weak spots, and considered the castle's drains as a distinct, if odorous, possibility.

It was believed that one of the drains that ran out of the main part of the castle was from the canteen. Nothing could be done during daytime and at night the canteen was locked. The hundreds of prisoners in the castle had between them an enormous range of skills, and this included the ability to manufacture keys. From pieces of an iron bed frame a key was made enabling them to enter the canteen at night and clamber down the drain – which they soon found ended in a four-foot thick brick wall. Working in shifts each night it took the men just a week to break through the wall. There, though, the drain stopped. Whilst it did not go as far as they would have wished, all that was needed was further tunnelling.

What was found was a bank of dense, sticky clay and further tunnelling would have been extremely difficult. Nevertheless, the end of the drain did come out beyond the castle walls and a vertical shaft up to the surface was dug. Pat Reid planned to cut his way through the last layer of earth and soil on the actual day of escape and then build a trapdoor which would be concealed from above with the large sod of grass he had cut away, so that the escape route could be used again in

Above: A view of Colditz Castle, the former *Oflag* IV-C, today.

Above: This part of *Schloss* Colditz served as the Guardhouse of *Oflag* IV-C. The main entrance to the inner, prisoners', courtyard can be seen on the right. (Historic Military Press)

the future. The only problem was that when the prisoners climbed out of the hole they were likely to be spotted.

Whilst thought was given to this issue, two Polish prisoners tried one night to hacksaw their way through one of the canteen's outside windows. They were spotted, or heard, by the patrolling guards and arrested. The consequence of this was that a bright floodlight was then placed outside the canteen which meant that there was little chance of getting into the canteen unobserved. The lock on the canteen door was also replaced with a far more sophisticated one.

These measures did not, nevertheless, end all hopes of using the canteen as an escape route. It simply meant a new method of entering the canteen would have to be found. The main problem facing any would-be escapers was that the trapdoor at the end of the tunnel came out where a guard was always on patrol. Until this problem could be solved, however, the canteen route was shelved.

Another likely opportunity to escape was when the prisoners were marched down to the park at the foot of the cliff outside the actual castle building for recreation. One day, as the prisoners were returning to the castle, at a pre-arranged signal the marchers distracted the guards whilst a French officer and a Polish officer slipped into the seldom-used basement of a house near the path. They intended to wait there until nightfall before making off in the dark. The men were not missed until the evening roll-call or *Appell*. An immediate manhunt was launched and the two would-be escapers were found.

Living in close proximity in the confines of the castle for long periods of time, it was inevitable that some of the guards and inmates established a degree of mutual trust. One friendly guard in particular began to smuggle small items of food into the camp for the prisoners who, in return, gave him items from their Red Cross parcels. It was realised by the Escape Committee, which had been formed by the prisoners to coordinate and combine their efforts, that this friendly relationship could be developed for a greater purpose. The guard was told that he could make some money if he turned a blind-eye for a few moments one evening. For the sum of 500 Reichsmarks, 100 of which were given in advance, at a given time on a given day he was simply to stand at the far end of his beat for ten minutes. This was quite permissible, so he could not be accused of doing anything to aid the escapers. What this meant was that the canteen tunnel could now be used, as the men would be able to get away during the ten-minute pause in the guard's beat. If they could open the canteen door, the tunnel escape was now entirely practical once again.

Twelve men, including four Poles, were to make the escape attempt whilst the guard was standing out of sight. Getting out of the castle was, however, only the first part of the escape, and in many respects the easiest part. Travelling hundreds of miles through German territory without being stopped and arrested was much more challenging. The Poles spoke German and knew the country quite well. They would be indispensable travelling companions.

For months the men in Colditz had been working on creating all the necessary clothing, papers and maps that any escapers would need. On the evening before the escape attempt, 29 May, all this material appeared, as Pat Reid described: 'From out of astonishing hiding places came trousers and slouch caps made of grey German blankets, multi-coloured knitted pullovers, transformed and dyed army overcoats, windjackets and mackintoshes, dyed khaki shirts and home-knitted ties. These were donned and covered with army apparel. Maps and compasses appeared.'[1]

Reid managed to hide in the canteen after it was closed for the day and he dismounted the new lock from inside. During *Appell* that evening he slipped out of the canteen and took his place in the ranks. As the prisoners broke up after the *Appell* the twelve escapers plus Reid sneaked quickly into the canteen.

They moved along the tunnel and up the vertical shaft. Reid, who, as Escaping Officer, was not himself allowed to escape (it being his role to facilitate and assist the escape of others), cut his way through the grass. He stood up into the fresh air, followed by Captain Rupert Barry. Then a shadow fell across Reid's crouching figure. That shadow was of a German officer brandishing a pistol. They had been rumbled.

Reid had already guessed that the friendly guard had deceived them and when Reid was led off to face *Hauptmann* Paul Priem (the principal camp officer at Colditz who was responsible for the administration and discipline of the PoWs) the German officer said that 'German sentries know their duty. The whole matter has been reported to me from the start … I had my men posted at all windows and beneath on the road. They were to shoot if any prisoners ran or struggled.'

The escapers were all caught in the tunnel and marched off to solitary confinement – though thirteen in a cell was hardly solitary. As for the guard, he was allowed to keep his 100 marks. He also was granted extra leave, promoted and received the War Service Cross![2]

The next opportunity that presented itself was not the product of months of preparation, but an entirely spontaneous event. A large lorry drove into the camp with some French prisoners who were held in Colditz town. They had been sent to collect a number of prison mattresses, or palliasses, which were stored above the Dutch quarters. These mattresses were little more than large sacks filled with straw and they were being taken into the town in preparation for the arrival of a batch of Russian prisoners who would be housed there.

The opportunity to smuggle one of the Colditz inmates onto the lorry was too good to miss. After a hurried discussion Second Lieutenant Peter Allen was chosen. He was only small and could speak German fluently.

He was given what clothing was available, some money and was hastily bundled into one of the sacks. Reid spoke to one of the Frenchmen to tell him what they were going to do and managed, after some persuasion and a packet of cigarettes, to enlist his support.

The Frenchman duly carried Allen over his shoulder and dropped him onto the pile of the rest of the mattresses. After some half-hearted prodding of the sacks by the camp guards, the lorry trundled out of the castle.

Peter Allen was soon dropped off in a deserted house in the town. He climbed out of a window and was off. He travelled as far as Vienna but, suffering problems with his legs, he was taken to hospital, where he revealed his true identity.

In April 1941, the first successful escape and 'home run' was achieved. A French prisoner, Lieutenant Alain Le Rey, chose to make his escape in broad daylight under the very noses of the guards. On 11 April, Good Friday, the men went down to the park for their usual period of exercise. On the way back up to the castle Le Rey slipped away from the group and into a disused building known as the Terrace House. The house was being repaired and the builders were storing their materials in a small room on the ground floor. This was where Le Rey hid away. As only two other men were aware of his escape plan, he knew that his absence was likely to be discovered at the evening *Appell* as there would be no concerted effort to confuse the guards when they were counting. Le Rey, therefore, had to make his break before nightfall.

A little after 18.00 hours, he broke cover and simply ran down the road. No-one saw him. He took the train, not only down to the Swiss border, but also across it. Le Rey was not the first prisoner to escape from the confines of Colditz, but he was the first of many to complete a 'home run'.

The second was another Frenchman, Lieutenant Réne Collin. Inspired by Le Rey's escape, Collin chose a similar method. Within the confines of the park was a pavilion. During the exercise period on 31 May 1941, Collin climbed into the rafters of the pavilion. The Germans knew Collin was missing but had no idea where he was. He remained there until nightfall when he made good his escape.

Amongst the few who knew how Collin escaped was Lieutenant Pierre Mairesse Lebrun, and, just over a week later, on 9 June, he attempted to replicate Collin's method. He too, was able to hide away until nightfall and escape. Lebrun, however, only had an old, 1928-dated 100-mark note, which had been sent to him by his family inside a nut in a pot of jam. It was out of date and no longer legal tender. He was caught trying to buy a ticket at the railway station.

One of the next attempts was foiled by British honesty and courtesy. This occurred on 25 June, the story later being told by Captain Kenneth Lockwood: 'We were coming back from the walk in the park, and we passed this lady, perfectly turned out, coming towards us in the opposite direction. Well, nobody bothered about it very much until [Squadron Leader] Brian Paddon looked down and noticed that she'd dropped her watch. So, being a gentleman he picked it up and ran after her but she just kept walking along. The guards who were with us saw this scene and then it suddenly occurred to them there shouldn't be a lady walking down here, so they ran after her. It was indeed no lady.' It was in fact Lieutenant E. Boulé.

The French continued to scheme and it was Lieutenant Lebrun who would, in his second escape bid, achieve the next home run – and this would be daring in the extreme. In the days leading up to his escape he spent as much time as possible running in the park to build up the muscles in his legs. On 1 July he sprung, quite literally, his plan.

As usual Lebrun began running the circuit of the park in his normal running gear. When he reached a particular spot a friend, Lieutenant Pierre Odry, was stood near the perimeter wire. Using his friend as a catapult, he ran, stepped into Pierre Odry's cupped hands and leapt clear over the ten-foot fence. Of course the Germans spotted him and as soon as they had recovered their wits, opened fire on the French officer. Lebrun was still not free as there was an eight-foot wall surrounding the park. Dodging bullets, he cleared the wall and escaped. Soon after he stole a bicycle and rode his way to the Swiss border. Two weeks later *Kommandant* Reinhold Eggers received a letter from Odry requesting the return of his personal effects!

The Polish Lieutenant J. Stepniak made his bid for freedom on 16 July from a nearby hospital where he had been sent. He was recaptured but not before he had got as far as Württemberg in southern Germany.

It was yet another French White Russian officer, Lieutenant Tatistcheff, who made the next home run, thanks to an affair of the heart.

In the town was a secondary, or lower, prison camp, the *Schützenhause*. It was not a high security prison and was not as heavily guarded as the main castle. It held a number of French officers and men who were opponents to the Communist regime in Russia and who had emigrated to France. These men were mostly members of the Russian Orthodox faith and were granted the special privilege of visits from the Orthodox bishop of Dresden at special times in their religious calendar. One of those events was on 17/18 July and the bishop duly arrived with a mixed male and female choir.

After the service, as the bishop and his entourage departed and the prisoners were taken back to their quarters, it was noticed that Tatistcheff was missing. It transpired that one of the women in the choir, a Miss Hoffman, had succumbed to the lieutenant's charms and helped him escape. Tatistcheff succeeded in reaching home, but poor Miss Hoffman was imprisoned.

There were an astonishing sixty-two known escape attempts during 1941 – more than one a week. Many were detected by the Germans before they were completed but this figure does give an indication of the scale of the problem facing Eggers and his men. Escapes were being planned or enacted almost the whole time.

Ten of those attempts were successful, including two that involved more than one man escaping. Four French lieutenants, Navelet, Charvet, Lévy and the man who had helped Lebrun vault over the park fence, Pierre Odry, feigned illness and were taken to the hospital at Elsterhorst. They hoped to find an easy way out of the hospital, which was attached to the French prisoner of war camp of *Oflag* IV-D. Finding all the likely exits well-guarded, the men recovered from their illness and, on 14 October, were taken back to Colditz under guard.

It was a march of three miles to Colditz and it was already dark. As the party walked through the Saxony countryside, it passed through some woods. Never was there a better opportunity. At the same moment, all four broke away in different directions. Navelet and Ordry reached home; Jacques Charvet and Rémy Levy were captured at Aachen. The latter pair was taken back to eastern Germany by train and on the way, Charvet jumped out and ran away. He was seen and tracked down, being eventually retaken at the border town of Helmstedt.

Another mass escape was the last attempt of 1941, taking place on 17 December. Eggers himself tells the story: 'That evening, a party of seven were sent down to the town dentist, five P.O.W.s and two guards, because in the *Schloss* the French officer dentist hadn't the material for more than simple fillings. The patients all came out of our dentist's house together after treatment. Their guard came last. It was very foggy and it was raining too that evening. Three of the party just bolted down the street. Lieuts. Durand-Hornus, de Frondevill and Prot. There was nothing the guard could do about it. He couldn't run three ways at once. He daren't fire blindly into the fog. We could do nothing more either once we had warned everyone. So back we went to our Christmas festivities, but the soup was cold and the spirit of the feast was much watered down.' All three made it back to France.

The first successful British home run came early in 1942. In this Lieutenant Airey Neave and Dutch Lieutenant Tony Lutejin (or Luteyn as he is also referred to) aimed to walk out of the castle disguised as German officers. Neave had spotted a little wicket gate by the castle moat. A path led through this gate to the outside world. If he was able to get as far as the moat he would be able to walk out of the castle grounds without having to pass through any of the checkpoints that guarded every other exit.

The Germans had allowed the prisoners to occupy themselves with shows in the upstairs theatre. The men, consequently, began to prepare a pantomime for the 1941 festive period. It was found that there was just enough room under the stage for the men to crawl and the prisoners soon began to saw away at the floor boards. The passage below was in the German quarters. Neave and Lutejin would obviously have difficulty trying to leave the prisoner quarters in German uniforms without arousing suspicion, or being challenged. However, what could be more natural than German officers walking out of the German quarters?

The next few weeks were taken up by Neave and Lutejin making their German uniforms. Eventually, they were ready and, on 5 January 1942, they dropped through the passage below the theatre into the German portion of the castle. Pat Reid went with them as far as the door to the outside to pick the lock. After an agonizing few minutes the door swung open, and the two men were out into the open. 'The testing time had come,' wrote Neave some years later. 'I strode through the snow trying to look like a Prussian. There stood the sentry, the fallen snow covering his cap and shoulders, stamping his feet, just as I had pictured him. He saluted promptly, but he stared at us, and as our backs were turned I felt him watching. We walked on beneath the first archway and passed the second sentry without incident. Then, between the first and second archways, two under-officers [i.e. NCOs] talking loudly came from the *Kommandantur* [the garrison office]. They began to march behind us. I felt Luteyn grow tense beside me. I clasped my hands behind my back with an air of unconcern. I might have been casually pacing an English parade ground. In a moment of excitement I had forgotten my part. "March with your hands at your side, you bloody fool," came a fierce sharp whisper from my companion.'

Finally they came to the little wicket gate. 'As Luteyn opened it I watched the under-officers, their heads bowed to the driving snow, march on across the moat bridge. Down we went into the moat, stumbling and slipping, until we reached its bed. A soldier came towards us from the married quarters. He reached us, stopped and stared deliberately. I hesitated for a moment ready to run, but Luteyn turned on him quickly and in faultless German said crossly: "Why do you not salute?"

'The soldier gaped. He saluted, still looking doubtful, and began to walk up the side of the moat towards the wicket gate. We did not look back but hastened up to the path on the far side, and, passing the married quarters, came to the high oak paling which bordered the pathway above the park. We were still within the faint glare of searchlights. Every moment that we stayed on the pathway was dangerous. Lifting ourselves quickly over the paling, we landed in thick snow among a tangle of trees. My cardboard belt was torn and broken and with it into the darkness went the holster.' Also into the darkness went both men, who each succeeded in making that perilous but exhilarating home run. Upon his return to the United Kingdom, Neave joined the branch of Military Intelligence devoted to assisting Allied servicemen escape German occupied territory, MI9.[3]

This route out through the hole under the stage and along the German quarters was tried again the following night. On this occasion, the potential escapees were a Dutch Lieutenant, H. Donkers, and Lieutenant John Hyde-Thompson. They did succeed in walking out of Colditz but they were recaptured at Ulm railway station.

The heavy snow falls that winter gave Flight Lieutenant F. Flinn another unorthodox escape idea – that of digging a tunnel through the accumulated snow on the canteen roof. He was detected and spent a month in solitary confinement. 'Errol' Flinn was a persistent escaper and being caught each time did not dampen his enthusiasm. By April 1943 Flinn would have amassed a total of 170 days in solitary confinement, almost half a year.

There was no let-up in escape attempts throughout 1942, but the next successful one after Airey Neave was not until April. This was when a Belgian, Captain Louis Rémy, escaped from the train station on his way to a military hospital at Gnaschwitz. According to Eggers, he 'just dashed away and was never seen again'. In fact he made his way down to the Mediterranean and reached a British ship off Algeciras, a port city in the south of Spain, and eventually made his way home.

Those prisoners who were taken out of Colditz clearly had greater opportunities for escape and this was certainly the case with Squadron Leader Brian Paddon. He had been involved in a number of failed escape attempts, including making a bid for freedom from the Gnaschwitz military hospital. He was on the run for some time before he was arrested at a train station. His travelling companion was a Polish officer called Josef Just. The Pole was wearing a distinctive khaki-green overcoat, which drew the attention of the railway police. Just's true identity was revealed when he was asked to take off his underpants. The label at the back read 'Lt J Just Oflag 4C'. Both men were returned to Colditz.

Because of this escape attempt and because in his previous prison of war camp, *Stalag* XX-A at Thorn, he had insulted a German NCO and accused him of theft, Paddon was due to be sent back there to face a court-martial. He was transferred to Thorn the day before his scheduled hearing. Paddon immediately looked for a means of escape. He saw that each morning gangs of prisoners went from the camp to work in the nearby fields. These work parties were only lightly guarded as, unlike the inmates of Colditz, the prisoners at Thorn were not considered to be high risk.

The prisoners assembled at 07.00 hours by the camp gates. Paddon's court-martial was due to start at 09.00 hours. He had just two hours to make good his escape. He told his fellow prisoners what he intended to do and they promised to help as far as they could.

Paddon joined the work party, having been given a battledress by the prisoners to cover the civilian clothes that he had worn on his train journey from Colditz, and marched with the others to the fields. At the first opportunity he slipped behind a haystack. He then struck off through woods and away. He had the address of a Polish officer's girlfriend in Danzig and, as he spoke fluent French, he made his way to the Baltic port posing as a Belgian worker.

'We never discovered how Paddon escaped,' conceded Eggers. 'We suspected that he had somehow joined a party of British orderlies, working in the prison, and had gone out with them on some job. Dogs followed a trail from one working party, having been given some of his clothing to sniff. The trail ended in a bog. Perhaps they thought that was the best place to report the last trace of this turbulent beast! Later, his comrades told us that he was home in England, having got there via Sweden.'

The earlier successful escapes through the German part of the castle indicated that there was a greater prospect of achieving a breakout from that side of the building. This was because the Germans did not expect that prisoners would, or could, be in that area. With this theory in mind, one British officer, Captain 'Lulu' Lawton, came up with an outrageous plan – to escape through one of the Germans' most secure rooms of all in the castle. This was the office of *Stabsfeldwebel* Gephard, known to the prisoners as 'Mussolini'. No-one would ever dream of prisoners entering, much less escaping from, that room. The difference with this room was that it was in the prisoners' compound. It was, though, unguarded, and someone exiting that room would have a comparatively easy passage to the outside.

Gephard's room was securely locked with both a standard lock and a cruciform lock. The prisoners had become experts at picking the standard locks but the cruciform locks were entirely different. Fortunately, one of the Dutch officers, Damiaem van Doorninck, whilst formerly a lecturer in cosmology and higher maths, was also an expert watch repairer. His skills soon became known to the Germans who also took their watches to him for repair. As a result, he had been permitted to assemble a small tool kit. One of these tools he used for gauging the teeth in a cruciform lock, and he was soon able to manufacture keys for every cruciform lock in the castle.

One night Pat Reid broke into the office to assess its potential. He saw that there was a widow, with bars, that overlooked the northern terrace of the castle where there was a shed used by the Germans as a storeroom. If they could tunnel from the *Stabsfeldwebel*'s office into the storeroom they would be outside the prisoner compound. From there they would dress up as workmen who often came up from the town and collected equipment from the storeroom. They would have two Polish officers dressed as the usual German escort and the whole party would then simply walk through the gates and away.

'The plan was designed to be executed over two nights,' Lockwood explained. 'On the first, I would pretend to be ill in the sick bay. Pat

Reid and Derek Gill would be hiding under my bed, and when all was quiet I would let them out of the sick bay and into Gephard's office. I would then lock them in.' Reid and Gill were to prise up the floorboards under Gephard's desk and make a hole in the storeroom wall, but not break through completely. The next night, 9 September, six men, three Dutch officers, including van Doorninck, and three British, sneaked into the *Stabsfeldwebel*'s office and completed the hole in the storeroom. Wishing to conceal the method of their escape, the prisoners not only carefully replaced the floorboards under Gephard's desk but also repaired and repainted the storeroom wall!

They were now ready to leave the storeroom but had to wait for the evening change of guard on the terrace, as the new sentry would assume the work party had entered the storeroom during the previous shift. All went well and the party left the store and marched down through the park to the large gate in the wall. The key master van Doorninck was responsible for opening this gate, but none of the keys he had manufactured fitted the lock. 'I turned around and immediately spotted a German NCO holding a huge key in his hand,' van Doorninck later recalled. 'I shouted at him: "Have you got the key?" "Yes – didn't you know that?" he replied. "No, we have only been in Colditz for a few days and at the main gate they told us we could get out by a shorter route through here."[4]

The guard accepted van Doorninck's explanation and duly opened the gate. They marched off down towards the town and, once they were out of sight of the gate, they slipped into the bush and stripped off their outer clothes. Only two of the party managed to avoid recapture and make home runs. One of these was Australian Flight Lieutenant Bill Fowler; the other was the master key smith himself, van Doorninck.

Without doubt, one of the most complex, and ingenious, escape attempts was that conceived by Lieutenant Albert Michael 'Mike' Sinclair, who, serving in the 2nd Battalion King's Royal Rifle Corps, had been captured in northern France in 1940. Sinclair was addicted to the 'escaping game', as his oldest companion Gris Davis-Scourfield recalled: 'I would wake up in the middle of the night, as we were usually in the same room. Mike would be standing at the window just watching the sentries patrolling below, counting the number of seconds it took them to turn around and walk back on their beats. He was constantly looking for information that might be useful to him.'

Sinclair's constant observing and thinking gave him the impetus for this next attempt, the idea for which he proposed in April 1943. It involved impersonating one of the best-known of the German guards, *Stabsfeldwebel* Fritz Rothenberger.

A decorated First World War veteran, Rothenberger was known to the prisoners and guards alike as 'Franz Joseph'.[5] His nickname arose because of his similarity with that of the late Austrian Emperor of the same name – ruddy complexion, puffy cheeks, grey hair, portly bearing and an enormous ginger-coloured, white-topped moustache which covered half his face. It was this last distinctive feature of the German NCO which leant itself to imitation.

One of Rothenberger's tasks each night, Sinclair had noted, was to inspect the sentries on the eastern terrace of the castle. He would undertake his rounds in the middle of the night to make sure the sentries were alert and vigilant. The terrace was guarded by men posted thirty yards apart. Once he had completed his tour Rothenberger would leave through the terrace gate, which was manned by two guards – one who patrolled the catwalk above, the other who stood by the gate to allow guards and other personnel to pass through.

The plan devised by Sinclair, now called the 'Red Fox' by the Germans, and Lieutenant Monty Bissell, was that Sinclair would impersonate Rothenberger and walk up to the two guards, telling them that there was a disturbance on the other side of the castle, and ordering them to hand over the gate key whilst they went back to the guardroom for further instructions. Whilst the guards were away, two prisoners dressed as Germans would take their place at the gate. Bissell and Sinclair had calculated that it would take four-and-a-half minutes for the sentry to march back to the guardroom, during which time twenty prisoners would swing down ropes from the castle windows and escape through the gate. If things went really well, a further ten would follow.

Obviously, the ruse would soon be discovered and then the guard and the real Rothenberger would come hurrying back. The two imitation guards would, by this time, also have taken off 'in pursuit' of the escapers. Though the Germans would know that something had happened, they would not know how many prisoners had got away nor which direction or directions they had taken. This would give the escapers a good chance of covering a reasonable distance the Germans could hope to begin tracking them down.

For it to succeed, the scheme obviously rested upon how well Sinclair could impersonate Rothenberger. The prisoners had often observed the way in which the Germans obeyed instructions without question and it was hoped that this deference to rank would mean that the guards would immediately obey the fake Rothenberger without daring to challenge him in any way. This was not just a case of stereotyping, as one of the Germans, Peter Hoffman, explained: 'We were proud of our Prussian traditions. We all thought Rothenberger was a real German soldier. He had fought in the First World War, he had an Iron Cross – and his moustache. Of course, if he ordered one of us young ones to do something we would certainly do it.'

To succeed, Sinclair's plan required considerable preparation. First of all, three German uniforms would be needed. As it was still cold at night, the Germans on duty wore greatcoats, so three of these were manufactured from blankets which then had to be dyed the exact colour of grey. The insignia worn on the coats were made out of linoleum cut from the floor and painted with watercolours purchased in the canteen shop.

Altogether some fifty men of the so-called 'Escape Academy' were involved in preparing for the escape attempt. One of the next tasks was to forge a copy of Rothenberger's Iron Cross which was prominently worn by the NCO. This was cast in zinc that had been stolen from the roof of the building. It was heated up on an open stove and was shaped with a broken table knife. Meanwhile, a replica of Rothenberger's hat was produced by the men who provided the theatre props for the plays and shows that the prisoners were allowed to perform. For this an RAF cap was dyed green and fitted with a peak.

Next, two artificial rifles had to be manufactured for the fake guards. This was done in wood with the use of a home-made lathe. The barrels of the 'rifles' were polished with lead pencils to give the appearance of metal, and both weapons were provided with scabbards for bayonets, whilst the 'guards' also wore a holster and revolver. The attention to detail was remarkable, with triggers for the rifles being cut out of tin and the rifle bolts being fashioned from the prisoners' metal bedsteads.

Rothenberger's pistol was a Walther P.38. Normally, of course, it was in its holster with just the black base of the magazine at the bottom of the handgrip being visible. So this was the only bit that had to be made. The holster itself was made from cardboard with stitching penciled on and dyed a dull red to imitate leather.

Whilst all this activity was taking place under the very noses of the Germans, Sinclair rehearsed his role as 'Franz Joseph'. He studied Rothenberger carefully as he strode around the camp, and under the considered eye of the Colditz theatre impresario, Lieutenant Teddy Barton, Sinclair practiced the German NCO's movements and mannerisms. Barton was also the man responsible for Sinclair's crowning glory – the great moustache. This he made out of shaving brushes. It took him fourteen attempts until he was happy that he had created a satisfactory replica. The two false guards, Lieutenant John Hyde-Thompson and Captain Lance Pope, who both spoke German, also had to learn their parts well, being able to mimic the German drill.

The scale of the prisoners' operation was astonishing, as it must be remembere that getting out of the camp was merely the first stage to success. Once the men were out into the German countryside they would each need authentic looking civilian clothes as well as a full set of papers. The latter were produced by the camp's forgery department. One of the forgers was Kenneth Lee: 'Every day we sat at a table opposite each other painstakingly copying the German Gothic script on the paper forms. We started in pencil then carefully went over the top of everything in Indian ink. The raw materials came from the canteen shop and I suppose it never occurred to the Germans that we might be able to use this for escaping purposes, they thought we were all drawing still lifes. There was always a stooge at the window to warn us if the Germans were coming. We had a special hide under the table to put our equipment in, and I think it took about ten seconds to cover everything up and do something else. I spent over three years in the forgery department and we were never rumbled.'[6]

Each pass had to bear a photograph of the individual carrying it. For this Major William Anderson built an imitation box Brownie camera out of an old cigar box with broken spectacles serving as the lenses. One of the German guards provided the film and developer, presumably in return for bribes of items from the Red Cross parcels which the prisoners received.

The preparations did not end there, as each escaper also needed a map. These were copied from the few that had not been discovered by the Germans when new RAF prisoners arrived – as maps were part of the RAF escapers' pack that each crew member was issued with.

The windows of the rooms where the prisoners were held were protected with iron bars and if the men were to escape through the windows the bars had to be cut beforehand. The windows were directly above the sentry on the terrace gate and so the cutting had to be carried out with the absolute minimum of noise. This painfully slow process was undertaken every night with the cut in each bar being disguised with boot polish each morning. The bars were left with just a slither of metal until the night of the escape when the final cut would be made.

The last item that was needed was a camp pass. At each checkpoint the pass had to be shown. For security reasons the colour of these changed every few days. As well as presenting his pass, anyone passing through a checkpoint would be asked the security code of the day, which was a number between one and fifty. Clearly, information on these could only be obtained at the last minute. So, when everything was in place for the mass escape, Flight Lieutenant Cenek Chaloupka, a Czech airman, would swing into action. 'Checko' Chaloupka was an expert in blackmailing the guards. He would begin by talking to them, giving them coffee and cigarettes. Then he would give them little presents for their wife of children; they would exchange photographs and relationships would develop.

Once the two were comfortable with each other, Checko would ask for something in return from one of them – such as the loan of a camp pass. If the guard refused, Checko would let it be known that the Camp Commandant would be informed that the guard had been accepting gifts from the prisoners. The poor guard would be hooked. Once he had handed over one valuable item he would be in real trouble if his superiors found out, so the guard had no choice but to keep on handing Checko whatever he asked for.

Finally, everything was in place. It had taken many months of hard and careful planning and preparation throughout the summer, but by the beginning of September 1943 all was ready. D-Day was set for the 2nd.

After the 21.00 hours *Appell*, when Rothenberger was reported to be safely in the guardroom, the would-be escapers left their quarters using a skeleton key. Having made their way down to the first floor, the three fake Germans were lowered into the Sick Bay.

'The escapers had cut the window grill in the toilet of the officers' sick bay,' noted one of Colditz's guards, George Schaedlich, 'and had, from this corner, which no sentry could overlook, climbed down a short rope, hidden by the shadow. They had come down the steps behind the pavilion so that Sentry 4 had to assume they had come from the guardhouse.'[7]

The story of that night's action was later recorded by *Hauptmann* Eggers: 'Round about midnight Franz Joseph [i.e. Sinclair] appeared on his usual rounds outside the castle walls, accompanied, however, by two sentries with slung rifles. He came to the last two of the guard posts on the east side of the castle. Here was the gate with the catwalk above it ... The height of the catwalk above the ground enabled him to look over the edge of the canteen terrace and survey what had till then been dead ground all along the foot of the building. The last two sentries, over the gate, and on the beat up to it, had been on duty for about twenty minutes.

'Franz Joseph dismissed the sentry below the catwalk with the remark, "Your relief is early tonight. We have had air-raid distant warning." The guard was replaced by one of the men who had come with Franz Joseph but did not himself move off towards the guardroom, waiting apparently for his mate on the bridge above the gate to be relieved too and come back with him.

'The Sergeant-Major [still Sinclair] then went up to the bridge and relieved the last sentry, replacing him with the second man he had with him. The catwalk sentry, having been relieved, descended the steps from the gate and was just about to march off when, for no reason he could later define, he decided to ask Franz Joseph for his Sergeant-Major's pass.'[8]

Some accounts state that it was at this point that Sinclair had, 'slipped up, by missing a particular mannerism of Frank Josef. He made the mistake of not looking both sides of the catwalk before crossing. This was immediately picked up the guard, who was more astute than he had been given credit for.'[9]

'For once someone obeyed the rules we had been trying to drill into our sentries for years,' continued Eggers, 'and obeyed it in spite of himself. "Are you daft?' asked Franz Joseph. 'Don't you know your own Sergeant?"'

Faced with the choice of either persisting with the stubborn guard, or making a run for it with his two colleagues, Sinclair decided to continue with the façade. He became increasingly annoyed with the sentry and soon started yelling at him. The latter, however, stood his ground.

'The pass seemed in order, but, nevertheless, the guard had a vague suspicion and pressed his warning bell,' recalled Eggers. 'He also covered Franz Joseph with his rifle and ordered him to put up his hands. Joseph cursed – not very fluently – but did indeed put his hands up. In due course a corporal and one man appeared from the guardroom in answer to the buzzer. Franz Joseph did not know the password when asked. The corporal drew his revolver and demanded Franz Joseph's. There was a struggle. The corporal swore later that Franz Joseph tried to draw his pistol [which of course was impossible].'

At this point confusion reigned, with the German guards running around in panic and the NCOs unsure of the allegiance of the men under their command or who to believe! Suddenly, a shot rang out.

'"Good God" said one of our three sentries present. "You've shot our Sergeant-Major",' concluded Eggers in his account. 'But it was Lieut. Michael Sinclair, in almost perfect disguise, who collapsed to the ground. The true Franz Joseph appeared next on the scene, having heard the shots.'[10]

As the guards ordered an immediate *Appell* in the courtyard, Mike Sinclair was initially left lying on the ground. He was not, however, seriously wounded and his determination to escape as strong as ever. It would, though, in time result in a vain attempt to replicate Lebrun's leap over the park wire. He did not get far before being shot and killed by the guards.

Chapter 2

The Colditz Cock

Born on 12 July 1916 at Whitstable in Kent, Flight Lieutenant Leslie James Edward Goldfinch, who was known as Bill, was the third pilot of a Short Sunderland flying boat, serial number T9048 of Coastal Command's 228 Squadron, which had been involved in the evacuation of British and Commonwealth forces from mainland Greece to the island of Crete in April 1941. On the 25th of that month, fifty-two men, all RAF personnel, were rescued by Goldfinch and his crewmates and flown to Kalamata, where a further twenty were picked up. The grossly overloaded Sunderland failed to get airborne on its first attempt, but after a five-mile run on its second attempt, it staggered into the air and headed for Suda Bay, Crete.[1]

Goldfinch and his crew were immediately ordered to return to Kalamata. As the aircraft attempted to land in the dark it hit an object in the water and rapidly sank. Goldfinch was one of four survivors from the crew of ten - Flying Officer Bristowe escaped unhurt and managed to get to Crete, whilst the others, the captain, New Zealander Flight Lieutenant H.L. Lamond, the fitter, Sergeant Davies, and Bill Goldfinch suffered injuries. Goldfinch was taken to a military hospital, only to be captured when it fell into German hands some days later.

It was in the hospital that Lamond and Goldfinch joined company with Flight Lieutenant John William Best, of 39 Squadron, who had force-landed his Martin Maryland on 8 May, also at Kalamata, due to shortage of fuel. Jack Best was born near Llangollen in North Wales on 6 August 1912. He moved to Kenya as a young man where he took up farming. When the war began in 1939, Best joined the RAF and was trained as a pilot.

Above left: Bill Goldfinch as a young boy. Leslie James Edward Goldfinch, who was known as Bill, was born on 12 July 1916 at Whistable, Kent. (Courtesy of Pam Smith)

Above right: Bill Goldfinch pictured whilst a schoolboy. He was a second lieutenant in the Royal Engineers (TA) from 1935 to 1939. (Courtesy of Pam Smith)

Right: After a whirlwind engagement, Bill married Pauline in 1941 – they are pictured here during the ceremony. After just two days together as husband and wife, Bill was posted away, not returning until after the war. (Courtesy of Pam Smith)

Above left: Bill Goldfinch in uniform. In conversation with Tony Rolt at Colditz, Bill recalled how he ended up serving in the RAF. 'I got mad keen on flying and aircraft design. That sent me into the RAFVR when I was twenty-one. It must have been about 1938 … I got called up when war started.' Before the war Bill had been a civil engineer in the Colonial Service and worked in the Gold Coast (now Ghana), before gaining employment with Salisbury City Council in Wiltshire. It was from the latter that he joined up. (Courtesy of Pam Smith)

Above right: Bill Goldfinch, on the right, pictured in Durban, South Africa, during his training. (Courtesy of Pam Smith)

In time, Bill Goldfinch, Henry Lamond and Jack Best were moved, first to *Stalag Luft* I at Barth, and later to *Stalag Luft* III at Sagan, some 100 miles south-east of Berlin.

In May 1942, Lamond, Goldfinch and Best engineered the first escape from the camp at Sagan by tunnelling beyond the compund's surrounding wire. The original plan was to get to an airfield, help themselves to a German aircraft and fly to Sweden, rather than the UK. 'The real danger of that was where do you land in England,' Best remarked, 'and the answer is you don't know where you are, so you land in the first field you find and then Farmer Giles comes up with a pitch fork and you might even be in imitation German uniform and a very undignified end a pitch fork would be.'[2] In preparation, the two men had supplied themselves with the German words to help identify the various 'taps,' controls and instruments.

The three prisoners successfully dug their way out of the prison camp and reached the airfield. There they hid until dawn, sheltering inside one of a number of glider trailers. In the morning a group of air cadets arrived and started flying training with the gliders. By good fortune the escapers had chosen an empty trailer, but it was a long, hot day of suspense, heightened every time the cadets approached their trailer, and it was not until the evening departure that they were able to breathe freely. Then it was found that all aircraft were securely locked in the hangars and could not be removed. Therefore the trio agreed to push on through the night on foot towards the River Oder, continuing to follow the railway east to Glogau, which was reached by dawn.

Here they found an unlocked boat and began to row downstream towards the Baltic – 250 miles away! Rather than wait for darkness to blanket the river, the three men set off in daylight; the owner of the boat soon discovered its theft and reported his loss to the police. As there was only two directions which the boat could have gone, it was easily found by the authorities and the three were recaptured. Seen as 'difficult' prisoners the three would-be escapers qualified for Colditz.

So we return to the winter of 1943 and Keith Milne's room where Bill Goldfinch was gazing out of the window over the confines of the *Schloss* and beyond. 'It was cold and the snow was falling,' he remembered. 'We were in a room with a window overlooking Colditz town, and the wind was blowing against the face of the castle. The snowflakes weren't coming down, they were actually drifting up and over the top. I watched the force of the wind at work on them, and what a smooth flow of air it was.'

What Bill Goldfinch had noticed was that the wind was not going round the castle but over it. The wind was blowing from the west and the snowflakes were moving, he estimated, at around five miles per hour. His mind went back to that day when he was sat in the glider trailer after escaping from Sagan.

Colditz Castle is a tall structure in itself and it sits on high cliffs. 'And

Above: Two Short Sunderland flying boats pictured moored in Messinia Bay off Kalamata while evacuating RAF personnel from Greece on 24 April 1941. In the foreground, and from which aircraft this picture was taken, is a Mk.I of 228 Squadron – T9048 coded 'DQ-N' – whilst in the background is a 230 Squadron aircraft, L2160, coded 'NM-X'. It was T9048 that Bill Goldfinch was flying in when it crashed two days later, leading ultimately to his capture. (Historic Military Press)

I thought this would be a perfect place to launch a glider. It would be like standing at the edge of a swimming pool, you could launch yourself into this rising air and float gently down. And that was it; that was Eureka. The French had dug tunnels under the chapel, others had gone through or over the wire. A few people walked through the gate. Airey Neave had gone out of the theatre. All of these places had been sorted and used. It seemed much simpler to me to just stand on the roof and jump off.'[3]

Goldfinch's eye then scanned the ground below for a landing strip and found it in the form of a grassy field across the River Mulde. This

Above: Short Sunderland T9048 being boarded by RAF personnel in a rowing boat off Kalamata, during the evacuation from Greece, 24 April 1941. (Historic Military Press)

piece of land was around 500 yards away – not an insurmountable distance considering the height of the castle.

The idea that then formed was to build a single-seat, skeletal-type glider, which would have just enough room to sit on a sloping-roof platform, and to hand-launch it into a strong wind. The proposal would have to be sanctioned by the Escape Committee and Captain David Walker was enlisted to present the idea. 'I think the audacity of it took their breath away,' remembered David Walker. 'They thought it was great. Even though we hadn't quite worked out the most crucial aspect.'

That crucial aspect was how to launch the glider as it would need, somehow, to be flung into the air with considerable velocity. Nevertheless, the seed had been sown in the inventive minds of the prisoners and a team of workers and security men was assembled. It was led by Lieutenant A.P.R. Rolt of the Rifle Brigade in conjunction with Goldfinch and Best.

The son of a brigadier, Anthony Peter Roylance Rolt was born at Bordon, Hampshire, on 18 October 1918, and brought up at St Asaph in Wales. He was educated at Eton, where he got into trouble for keeping a car, then went to Sandhurst before being commissioned into the Rifle Brigade. Rolt, recalls Jack Champ, himself a former Colditz PoW, was 'tall, good-looking and exuded good humour and friendliness'. He had achieved a degree of fame before the war as a motor-racing driver having won at Le Mans some years earlier.

In May 1940, Rolt, known to all as Tony, arrived at Calais, commanding a scout platoon, just as the Germans were appearing. Rolt – who was later to be awarded a Military Cross for his gallantry during the defence of the French port – gave first aid to a wounded soldier while firing his Bren gun to keep the enemy at bay, and later found

---

Below: Bill Goldfinch pictured sat behind Flying Officer John Lylian in early 1941. Lylian was killed in the crash of Sunderland T9048. (Bill Goldfinch via the John Evans Collection)

Above: When the war began in 1939, John William Best joined the RAF and was trained as a pilot. During one of his flights across Africa in 1941, his aircraft, a Martin Maryland Mk.II medium bomber of 39 Squadron, ran out of fuel off the coast of Greece during a reconnaissance flight in April 1941. This picture shows 39 Squadron Marylands undergoing servicing on a landing ground in the Western Desert as another aircraft returns from a reconnaissance flight.

---

himself on the other side of a concrete wall to a large party of Germans. On slipping away, he ran into British troops waving white flags and was quickly captured. Rolt's first attempt to escape was made while he was being marched away. He jumped into a ditch, then headed into a wood, but was soon apprehended once again.[4]

This was the first of many escape attempts, as one account reveals: 'Incarcerated at Laufen camp, he took part in a tunnel attempt which was discovered; he was then moved to Biberach, where he was in a four-man team that walked out of the prison gates dressed as workmen. Once outside the escapers had only the clothes they wore, and, thirsty and hungry, were within sight of the Swiss border when they ran into a guard with an Alsatian. Rolt and his companion were locked up in a cell with two Frenchmen before being returned to Laufen and put in solitary confinement.

'On being transferred to Posen, Rolt was involved in a plan to throw ladders across a moat, but the ploy was discovered during a practice attempt. He was then sent to Warburg, where an attempt to escape while dressed as a plumber failed when a guard discovered that he spoke no German. He was one of five men masquerading as Swiss civilians who cleared the gates but were arrested by a patrol which had spotted them on a train. Rolt's next escape attempt was from Eichstätt, where he was in a party dressed as members of a German general's entourage; they got two miles from the camp before being discovered.'[5] By this time, Rolt's determination and persistence had more than earned his promotion to Colditz, where he finally arrived in July 1943.

As the idea behind a possible glider escape developed, against the background of the hardships and depravations endured by the prisoners, Bill Goldfinch took on the role of aircraft designer. He worked in close collaboration with Jack Best, who was in charge of construction, in which capacity he made good use of his youthful experience on his father's farming and timber estate in Wales, prior to emigrating to Kenya.

Pat Reid described Goldfinch and Best as 'probably the two finest craftsmen in the camp', and of Goldfinch he said: 'His inner strength, the peculiar tough fibre which has nothing to do with physical strength, but a lot to do with mental equanimity, only made itself felt after long contact with his personality. He was the type of man who would survive in a lifeboat after weeks of exposure, long after the other occupants had gone overboard.'

Given the name 'The Colditz Cock', the aircraft was designed as a strutted, parasol-wing glider. The design was original, except that the rudder shape was based on the pre-war Luton Buzzard, as it was considered that this was a proven control.

In the library at Colditz there was actually a copy of the book *Airframes, Part II* by Cecil Hugh Latimer-Needham. 'Gliders in those days looked like aeroplanes without engines,' Goldfinch explained. 'So the shape was straightforward. What I really needed to know was how long and wide to make the wings.' The answer was provided by Latimer-Needham. Why such a book was in the library has never been explained, but nothing could have served the PoWs' purposes better. From this book Bill Goldfinch produced highly-detailed drawings.

The glider was to have a wingspan of thirty-three feet and, with its intended crew of two on board, would weigh 560lb. If propelled from the roof of the castle at thirty-one miles per hour into a headwind, it was believed that the glider would be able to fly the 500 yards to the open stretch of grass.

The security team, the 'stooges', comprised roughly forty men and was initially under the control of Captain David Walker. In time, Walker was replaced by Lieutenant Geoffrey Wardle, a Royal Navy submariner who had made a getaway in September 1942, only to be recaptured the next day.

Construction of the glider started at the beginning of 1944 with the provision of a suitable workshop. It was planned to manufacture as many of the smaller wooden parts under the security of the individuals' rooms. When the time came for the assembly of the glider, and the coverings of the wings and fuselage, the entire operation would be moved to another, at that time undetermined, place. The codename for the project was 'Heavy Industry'. This it undoubtedly was, occupying at its height half of the British officers in the prison as lookouts or workers.

How this lookout system worked was detailed by Jack Champ. 'There were four main living quarters in Colditz and each could only be reached from the courtyard through a narrow doorway, from where one climbed a spiral staircase to the three floors used for living quarters and eventually to the fourth floor which was used for study and recreation. Should a German enter the doorway the first British officer to see him would shout at the top of his voice, 'Goons up!' This cry would be echoed through the quarters so that within seconds everyone knew there were Germans about. This gave plenty of time for any nefarious activity to be halted and escape gear and tools quickly concealed in well-prepared hideouts.'[6]

Two garret storeys in the roof above the British sleeping quarters, over the chapel, were vacant and unused and the end part of the topmost floor, which was eighty to 100 feet long, was to be partitioned off and camouflaged to supply a workshop roughly ten feet by thirty feet at floor level. The author Andy Russell details what followed:

'The only remaining problem was the false wall. It would have to be built in one night to lessen the risk of detection. An exact drawing of the real wall was made and reproduced in sections made from three-

Above: RAF prisoners of war pictured in *Stalag Luft* III, Sagan, in the spring of 1942. On the right is Bill Goldfinch, whilst second from left is Jack Best. It is believed that the individual standing on the left is Flight Lieutenant (later Wing Commander) Henry Lamond – the main pilot of Sunderland T9048 when it crashed. (Courtesy of Pam Smith)

Below: A group shot of Allied prisoners of war at *Oflag* IV-C at Colditz Castle. Jack Best is standing on the very left of the back row, whilst next to him, wearing a scarf, is Bill Goldfinch. (Courtesy of Pam Smith)

ply and cardboard. Canvas was stripped from palliasses on beds in the unused dormitories. Plaster was applied to the canvas to match the wall of the attic. Here, the debris from the old French tunnel escape attempt (under the Chapel) came in handy, since obviously the plaster had been made from the same local ingredients.

'From the debris, they sifted fine grit, and mixed it with clay, fine sand and a little cement. The resulting mixture was slapped onto the canvas, supported on a framework of floorboards. It had already taken a fortnight to assemble the sections of the false wall, and collect enough cobwebs, soot and dust to help with making paint and whitewash as well as the plaster. Twelve men worked furiously through the chosen night, with shaded lights, screwing the framework to the ceiling trusses and then screwing the sections of false wall to it. The plastering was the last job, and it was fast approaching dawn: they had finished with enough time to apply professional touches to it, in case any Germans ever approached close enough to peer at it.

'As the early light filtered through gaps in the roof tiles, they stepped back to inspect the plastering, and realised it was the wrong colour! Dark brown, patchy, streaked with soot. But there was nothing they could do about it: the 7 a.m. roll call was almost upon them. Dick Howe was convinced the colour would change when the plaster dried out. The next night the plaster was inspected again, and was a slightly better colour. The next day, the Germans checked the attics … and noticed nothing wrong. And that night even Heavy Industries Ltd. could not tell the difference between the real and the false. The Colditz glider had its workshop at last!'[7]

Entry into the 'workshop' was gained by means of a ladder and a camouflaged trapdoor. To enter the workshop one man would sit on another's shoulders, remove the trapdoor lid and pull down the short ladder. Despite all the efforts at concealment, the trapdoor was discovered by one of the Germans, as Jack Best recalled: 'One of the German workmen came to me very excited one day. My knowledge of German is nil but it was perfectly obvious that he'd discovered the trapdoor, but hadn't seen the glider workshop. I got hold of Checko [Chaloupka] and said, "For God's sake fix it." Checko gave him seven hundred English cigarettes … I was nervous, I never trusted a bribed man. Then quite by chance, the man died a fortnight later.'

Jim 'Ginger' Rogers described this false room which he saw being created in the attic space: 'One Sunday afternoon, when all was normally quiet, the attic was the scene of feverish activity while a gang erected a prefabricated, wooden-framed, bed sheet-covered false wall at the western end and covered it with plaster made of old dirt, dug out by the French from their tunnel and stored conveniently in the attic, mixed with concrete. The mixture was carefully gauged as to become the same colour as the original wall when dry.

'For a few days after the wall had been built there was anxiety that the colour and smell of the wet plaster would give away the work, but the Germans never noticed the smell or, in the half-light (for there was no electric lighting in the room), that their long attic had been reduced in length by about twenty feet.'[8]

This remarkable room was also described by Jack Champ who was one of those who would sew the materials for the wings and fuselage of the glider: 'The wall on the right is false. The other side of it is an exact replica of the one you see on your left. We made it look the same so that when the Germans enter from the other end, having just come from the room below, they don't realise that the wall is false or that the room below us is now in effect 10 feet longer. The distance deceives the eye. They [the guards] seldom come up this far anyway, and to date it has worked perfectly … the end wall formed one end of this particular section of the castle and when the time came this wall, which was brick but very old, would be bashed down. The wings would be clipped into place on either side of the fuselage and they would be ready to go.'[9] Because there was no lighting in the room, tiles were removed from the roof to let the sunlight in, and replaced when the room was not in use.

Stairs to this garret were situated at the other end of the building and a glance through the door was sufficient to satisfy a visiting guard as to the non-existence of any untoward activity, without the need to walk to the far end, sixty feet away, although on one occasion the guards approached the false wall and tapped it. It sounded disturbingly hollow to the prisoners but the Germans were evidently untroubled.

A complete set of carpenter's tools was improvised by Jack Best, displaying the same incredible ingenuity that had produced Franz Josef and his German guards. A side-framed saw, or hacksaw, was required to cut the wooden wing spars and other wooden components. This was made with a handle of beech wood shaped from a bed board with a frame from an iron window bar, and a blade with eight teeth was made from a gramophone spring. For the finer woodwork a smaller saw was needed. This had the same structure except the bedspring blade had

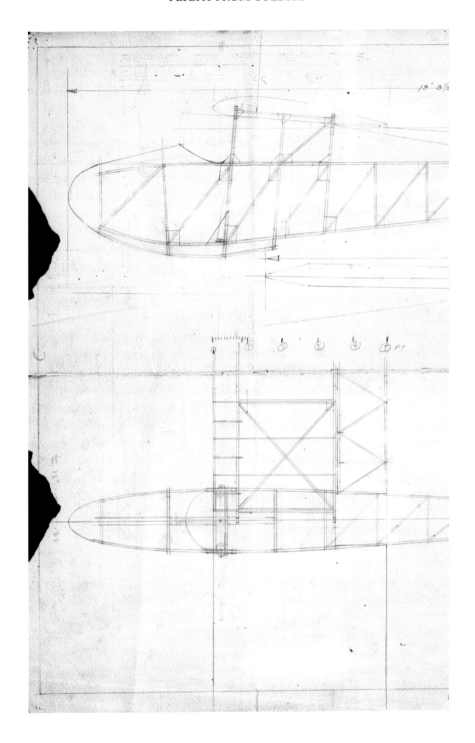

twenty-five small teeth. Jack Best described how he made this implement: 'The best saw I had was made out of the spring of an old gramophone. I cut teeth into it every sixteenth of an inch then tempered the blade in red-hot sardine oil on our stove. It was mounted on a frame stolen from a window bar.'

Once roughly cut, the wood had to be planed down. A large, fourteen-and-a-half-inch plane was made by fixing four pieces of bed board together to form a box into which was then fitted a two-inch blade that had been bribed from one of the Guards. A smaller plane (eight-and-a-half inches long) was similarly fashioned, but with a blade made from a table knife liberated from the canteen. The smallest plane of all, just five inches long overall, was also made with a gramophone spring. For drilling holes a drill of ⅝-inch metal was obtained again by bribing one of the guards, whilst bradawls were made from long nails. Iron bars from stoves became hammers. As the prisoners were unable to effectively drill metal, this meant that all of the fittings which required holes had to be sourced from pieces of metal located around the castle that had pre-existing holes in them in approximately the correct positions – though the holes could be enlarged with a round file.

'We would spend a lot of time wandering about looking for a piece of metal of a certain shape with the hole in the right place,' remembered Goldfinch. 'I can remember once walking round the courtyard with Tony saying "look it's going to be thousands of little bits of wood [and] we have got to stick them all together and we shall need some glue".'[10]

Amber-coloured German animal glue in the form of pellets, and various metal pins, were obtained by barter, mostly by 'Checho' Chaloupka. 'We might have called the glider *Amber*,' said Bill Goldfinch, 'because that's what held it together'.

Finally, an accurate gauge was made from pieces of bed board, a cupboard bolt and a gramophone needle.

The wing spars, of rectangular or plank section, a quarter of an inch thick, and the longerons, were made, each in one length without needing to splice pieces together, from floor boards of an inch or so in thickness, whilst most of the secondary structure material came from bed-boards. Asked what happened when the Germans discovered some

---

Opposite: The first plans of the 'Colditz Cock', which were drawn in pencil on artist's paper by Flight Lieutenant Bill Goldfinch. (IWM; EPH3117)

of the floorboards were missing, Goldfinch stated: 'The Goons just had to make the necessary repairs.'

Thirty-two ribs were made for the wings and the tailplane. The ribs were put together in jigs, dovetailed, glued and gusseted, where necessary using three-ply wood stripped down to two-ply, and then nailed into position. The underside of the wing was flat. The curve on the upper leading edge was reproduced on the aerofoil sections partly by bending the wood strips and partly by making a series of small saw nicks along the outer edge to give pliability. Pat Reid explained how the aerofoil sections were assembled, which was by threading on to the spars and tacking into position.

'The fuselage itself was constructed from floor-boards cut into strips of section one-and-a-quarter inches by three-quarters of an inch,' Reid continued with his explanation. 'The two side trusses were curved in both the vertical and horizontal planes and were strapped together at the bottom by short, straight ties and at the top by longer hooped ties, all gusseted where necessary. A raised head-rest, behind the pilot's seat, provided the pillar which supported the wings. Light wooden struts nine feet long were also used underneath the wings. A wide skid of well-planed board shaped like a ski was hinged to the fuselage at the front end. It was also highly polished with French chalk and lead. The top of the fuselage bellied upwards, which gave it a streamlined, airworthy appearance. It was not unlike the body of a Spitfire. The controls – stick, rudder-bar and rudder –were of conventional pattern, lightly constructed. The control wires were made from field telephone wire which the Goons had used for electric lighting in certain rooms.'[11]

Altogether, 6,000 pieces of wood, each of a specific length and width, many of them no bigger than a matchstick, were manufactured.

'Our greatest challenge was to find four "spars" with which to construct the wings,' recalled Jack Best. 'These needed to be sixteen feet long and preferably without a single knot in them. Eventually we found two perfect pieces in the *Saalhaus* right next to the German gateway. We couldn't just carry sixteen-foot pieces of wood across the yard, so we tacked them to a rather large table top, and then invented a reason to carry the table across the courtyard.

'When we got them into the workshop they were half-an-inch too thick, so we made a cut every inch of their length, then just chipped away at them with the "pranger", a table knife, broken off near the handle. Then we had to plane them.'

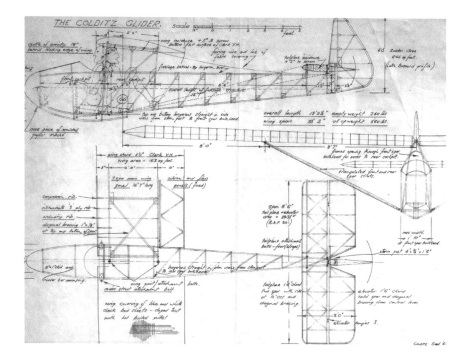

Above: An annotated set of drawings for the 'Colditz Cock' dated
September 1944. (Colditz Castle)

The age and condition of the timber were unknown quantities and
therefore specimens were subjected to bend tests. These gave the
surprisingly high figure of about 10,000lb/square inch. Each prisoner
was given a mattress and mattress cover, and it was this blue and white
check material which was used for covering the wings and fuselage – it
may be recalled that it was inside one of these very mattress covers that
Lieutenant Peter Allen made his escape in 1941.

The prisoners tended to prefer to take the covers off and sleep inside
the covers with a blanket thrown over the top. Some weeks from the
start of the 'Heavy Industry' operation volunteers had been asked to
give up their mattress covers – a very considerable sacrifice in an old,
cold castle.

Good quality beech plywood was obtained from cabinets in the
favoured senior officers' quarters, the *Saalhaus*, but as this was about
3mm thick one of the outer layers was peeled off for such items as rib

gussets, which were brackets that gave strength to the angle between the rib and the wing. The bolts for wing and lift-strut attachments came from the senior officers' beds and metal fittings were made from heavy gauge sheet from which the cabinets already mentioned were formed. The door hinges served as control hinges. As mentioned, field telephone cable, used as lighting conduit in the castle, served for the control cables. Squadron Leader 'Lucie' Lockett was responsible for manufacturing all of the metal fittings.

Jack Champ described how the fabric for the wings and fuselage was produced: 'We sat on the floor cross-legged like old fashioned tailors and sewed and sewed. The wing was constructed in conventional fashion with spreaders of varying lengths connecting to the outer section. We used large needles and strong thread and we carefully pulled the cotton "fabric" into place as we slowly worked our way along the edge.'[12]

By the end of September 1944 the sewing was completed but the cotton they had used was flimsy stuff and some method had to be found of stiffening the material. This was done by treating the fabric with dope made from boiled millet. The millet, which formed part of the food ration and was ground fine, was boiled in water for four hours to form a paste and then applied hot. As this made the fabric drum-tight for only about twelve hours, re-doping was to have taken place shortly before the launch.

As the space in the workshop was only seven feet across, the wings and the body had to be made separately, only to be put together before take-off. This meant a very high degree of accuracy in construction as there would only be one chance to get everything to fit together precisely.

Opposite top: A view of the upper attic above the Chapel at Colditz Castle. It was in this space that the prisoners had their original workshop and where they erected the partition behind which the glider was built. Note the skylight at the top of the roof from which the prisoners kept a look-out for the guards in the courtyard. (Keith Rodgerson)

Opposite bottom: In this picture of the upper attic the white line on the floor denotes where the prisoners' partition was located. It is beyond the line, therefore, that the PoWs had their concealed workshop for constructing the glider. (Keith Rodgerson)

Above: A view of what was the prisoners' courtyard at Colditz.
(Historic Military Press)

Below: Looking at the rear of *Schloss* Colditz. The grass area bottom right formed part of the PoWs' exercise area. (Historic Military Press)

The build of the Colditz Cock was undertaken by four prisoners at a time working in shifts in the glider workshop. One of these men watched at the door and received messages from three other 'stooges' who were looking out for any movement on the part of the German guards. Jack Best described the system of passing on messages: 'They had three coloured tin bottles. One was everything is OK, one was keep quiet there are Germans nearby, and another one was utter danger they are coming up your stairs.'

At first the man at the door watched for an hour before being relieved, but an hour of acute concentration was too long, and thirty-minute shifts became the norm. The stooges had to be very astute men. There was one on watch twenty-four hours a day and at any one time would know not only how many Germans were on duty but also who they were. The Germans were fully aware that they were being monitored but could not tell which prisoners were observing them so closely. In the end, according to Jack Best, the Germans learnt 'to live with it,' and 'used to come up [to the prisoners] and report on and off duty!'

Perhaps the biggest problem that the would-be escapers of Operation 'Heavy Industry' faced concerned the launch into flight from a complex of buildings, all with sloping roofs. The solution to this dilemma called for even greater ingenuity than the actual construction of the glider itself. Somehow a flat launching platform would have to be erected on the roof of the castle. 'It would be a hell of a gamble to get this platform built. Admittedly up on the roof we would be out of reach of the searchlights, but it would be dark [when work was done on the platform], we might have dropped something or someone may have fallen off,' observed Bill Goldfinch.

The roof of a second and lower building beside the 'workshop' was finally selected by Tony Rolt as the launching site. Roughly sixty feet long, the choice of this structure for the take-off still necessitated the construction of a wooden trestle runway, about four feet wide, saddling the whole length, which was to be prefabricated in sections. It so happened that the ridge could not be seen from the ground and this would have considerably simplified the task of building the platform unobserved at the requisite time. Under the prisoners' plans, on the night of the launch a hole would be punched in the workroom wall just at the level of the peak of the lower roof. The nose of the fuselage would be put out through the hole and the wings attached.

Above: The Lower Attic space at Colditz, which was immediately below the upper attic. This is the room from which the prisoners intended to take the glider out on to the roof during their final escape attempt.

The next question to be considered was how to provide the propulsive thrust to actually launch the glider into the air. The plan for this was to have the glider mounted on a launching trolley. The manufacture of this became the responsibility of Major Dick Lorraine, a peacetime civil engineer from Bristol. According to Pat Reid's version of events in his *The Latter Days at Colditz*, the plan was for a pulley to be positioned at the outer end of the platform and a 'rope' of lightning-conductor cable attached to the trolley was to pass over the pulley with a bathtub filled with concrete, to be made from tons of rubble (still stored from an audacious tunnel attempt by the French), suspended from the free end and thus providing a catapult-launch run of forty feet or so.

Pat Reid had escaped from Colditz by this time and his information was second-hand. Bill Goldfinch, in a taped interview, dismissed this method of propulsion, saying that this had been 'added' by Reid: 'I can't remember having a bath, we had showers. To fill a bath with concrete

Above: The only picture known to exist of the real 'Colditz Cock'. It is seen here in the Lower Attic in Colditz Castle having been photographed following the castle's liberation. (NARA)

would have meant doing it in the position that you were going to leave it. You simply would never have been able to lift it.'

Bill then explained how they had intended to launch the glider: 'What we did have in haul weight was people. We had hundreds of people and when the fire brigade go out and they are on the top floor they come down a pole don't they, well something like that. Ten people at 180lbs would have done it, but as we were all a bit thin it would have taken fifteen people, but that would have done it, and alongside was the clock tower, with a long drop down to the bottom.' As he also mentioned, the men would be travelling very fast by the time they hit the bottom, 'but someone could have arranged some mattresses as a buffer'. Jim Rogers said that he saw the rope being made: 'This was a fully engineered job, with rotating spools and races.'

The launch was planned to take place during an Allied air raid on Berlin or Leipzig, which were becoming increasingly frequent throughout 1944. Nevertheless, schemes for deadening the thud of the bathtub, or for the soft landing of the jumping prisoners, as well as for providing diversionary noises, formed part of the plot.

Positioning the glider for the launch meant first cutting a hole in the garret floor, through which the parts were to be lowered for pre-assembly, and then a second opening through the gable end by the roof platform. The lift-struts were to be hinged to the wing panels so that assembly merely meant connecting the wings to fuselage and raising them to allow the lift-struts to be pinned to the fuselage and adding the tail units.

A model of the Colditz Cock was made by 'Hoofy' Barnes to test the flight characteristics and this was audaciously launched from one of the upper windows into the courtyard below. In the words of Bill Goldfinch, 'it glided in beautifully to land at the feet of the Goon on guard'. There was even a plan, by Lieutenant 'Scarlet' O'Hara, to produce a petrol engine for increased range, but this project never got under way.

Colditz Castle is situated on the spur of a hill, which conferred the advantage of initial height for the launch. Meanwhile, the chosen landing area, beyond the castle boundary, was alongside, or even in, the River Mulde, some 300 feet below and 300-500 yards distant, where it curves away from the castle towards the northwest, and which would provide a landmark even on the darkest night.

Construction of the glider proceeded steadily throughout 1944 and was completed by the end of the year, when 'the stage was set for the greatest escape in history', to quote from Pat Reid's *The Latter Days*. However, when the Normandy landings took place, the advisability of continuing had been questioned, and its future was again reviewed upon completion, when a coded order from the War Office requested no further escape attempts in view of Hitler's orders for all recaptured prisoners to be shot out of hand. However, Colonel 'Willie' Tod (Royal Scots Fusiliers), the SBO or Senior British Officer at Colditz, decided that the glider should be held in reserve in case it became necessary to dispatch an emissary to contact the Allied forces.

The two glider escapers had not been selected, but, of the four leaders, Wardle had become an Escape Officer, which precluded him from taking part, and it is pretty certain that the choice would have fallen on Bill Goldfinch and Tony Rolt, with Jack Best as reserve pilot. The final decision, though, was to be made on the actual day of the flight.

Above: Newly-liberated Allied prisoners of war pictured on a bank outside Colditz Castle following the arrival of US troops on Sunday, 15 April 1945. The former captives were first allowed to venture out into the town the following Tuesday; the next day they began their journey home, being taken by truck to Kaledar airfield near Chemnitz. Sitting in the centre almost at the top of the bank, his pipe in his mouth, is Douglas Bader. To Bader's lower right is Bill Goldfinch. (Courtesy of Pam Smith)

Events beyond Colditz's walls moved very rapidly in the early part of 1945. As Soviet forces continually pushed further south and west, American and British troops were moving steadily east towards, and into, Germany. On the night of 13/14 February 1945, the prisoners witnessed a long and heavy air raid on Dresden just thirty miles to the north-east of the castle. This, the most devastating attack of its kind during the war with Germany, seemed to presage the end of German resistance. The guards realised that the end was imminent – as did the townsfolk of Colditz. According to Eggers, the ordinary townsfolk openly mocked officers in the street who still wore Hitler's uniforms.

The month of March was one of almost incessant aerial bombardment, with the cities of Germany being bombed and shelled into rubble. This inevitably meant that communications were badly disrupted throughout the country and food became increasingly scarce. There were discussions between prisoners and German officers about the advisability of evacuating Colditz. This would have meant the men walking into a war zone – something which was opposed by the prisoners. Such concerns prompted the prisoners to consider, once again, escaping and making a run for the advancing American forces. A number of successful escapes were made but these were comparatively conventional affairs. For its part, the Colditz Cock was never put to the supreme test of its hazardous nocturnal flight and it remained fast in its castle fortress until Colditz was liberated.

It was the Americans who arrived first. An account by the Australian War Memorial provides the following detail: 'On 14 April the German Commandant received an order to also remove the British prisoners from the castle … Lieutenant Colonel William Tod, refused. The inmates knew the end of their captivity was near and did not want to be moved. As neither the Commandant nor his superiors were willing to take responsibility for forcing the prisoners to leave at gun point, they remained in the camp. That afternoon, the shelling of the town began.

'The prisoners in the castle laid out a huge homemade Union Jack in the courtyard and spelt out PoW with sheets, in the hope the American reconnaissance aircraft would spot them, and the castle would not be shelled. Another Union Jack, and the French flag, were also hung in the camp.

'Unfortunately, the Americans did not initially see the flags or makeshift signs. On 15 April their artillery ranged on Colditz Castle and let off some small rounds. They believed the castle housed the remainder of the German garrison and did not realise it was a PoW camp. The castle's windows gave excellent views of the battle, and the prisoners cheered as they watched events unfold. However, with the Americans ranging on the castle, the prisoners were ordered to the cellars for safety … Luckily, before the shelling began in earnest, an American soldier spotted the French flag, and upon enquiries discovered the castle was a PoW camp.

'On 16 April, at 8am, the Americans advanced towards the castle, crossing the bridge [in the town] and liberated the prisoners of Colditz. The inmates were not completely free, however. For their own security they remained in the camp until arrangements could be made to evacuate them safely.'[13]

The same afternoon that the prisoners were liberated, the glider was assembled and a long queue formed to inspect the strange bird in their midst, including many of the PoWs, a number of American soldiers and some of the astonished German ex-guards who were themselves now captives.

So ingenious was the glider project that it soon made headline news. The *Derby Daily Telegraph*, for instance, published an article on Thursday, 19 April 1945, loosely based on information provided by Douglas Bader who had arrived at Colditz in 1943, though it contains inaccuracies as the reader will observe: 'Once, Bader and some of his friends tried to build a glider, to be launched from the roof, but the Germans caught onto the plan. "That sounds silly to you people who have been outside," he said, "but to those of us inside, it wasn't, because any means of escape was better than sitting around doing nothing".'

As C.H. Latimer-Needham observed in 1968, 'It is a soldier's duty, when captured, to take all reasonable steps to escape and, as is well known, the British PoWs fulfilled this duty in good measure. But of still greater importance is the avoidance of loss of morale and it is endeavours of this sort, which tax human ingenuity, improvisation and skill to the utmost, that make such valuable contributions to the sanity of an active body of men who suffer from the extreme frustration of immobility and inactivity at a time when their services are so sorely needed. By keeping forty or fifty men fully engaged over a period of some twelve months or so, the Colditz Cock served this purpose well.'[14]

It is believed that the glider was broken up and used for firewood by the inhabitants of Colditz; but one component, the rudder, was preserved in the local museum.

The Colditz Cock passed into legend. It was the subject of a TV film in 1971, *The Birdmen*, and it featured in one of the episodes of the BBC TV series, *Colditz*. There was even an Airfix model kit of the glider which was produced in the 1970s. So, it seemed, that was the end of this remarkable tale. Or was it?

Part Two

Chapter 3

The Challenge

It was just a normal August working day in 2011 when, in my Sussex workshop, I received a call from a television production company researcher with what sounded like an improbable suggestion. I have always been one for interesting and possibly too stressful challenges and the one proposed by the researcher was most certainly that. Being only two years into my own glider repair and construction business, a high profile project was going to be a major venture, but also one that would promote my company.

I had formed South East Aircraft Services in 2009, primarily to serve the gliding industry, but also the powered aircraft fraternity, through maintenance, modifications and repairs. I now mainly carry out wood and fabric restorations on vintage 'permit to fly' aircraft, as well as painting and finishing of new build kit aircraft for customers. I also service a number of wartime types for private individuals.

Success would certainly bring about notoriety and cement ourselves further into the industry as a significant player; failure would most likely undo everything my colleagues and I had worked hard to establish up to that date. The initial project brief was to the point; assess the likelihood of being able to recreate a full-size Colditz glider replica in the very roof of the former prisoner of war castle and launch it over the town to a hopefully successful conclusion in the fields alongside the river. All of this to be filmed for a TV documentary. The project was open for tender to several companies. I did not know who else had been approached, but with my interest in the Second World War I wanted this project personally and was prepared to do all that I could to make it happen.

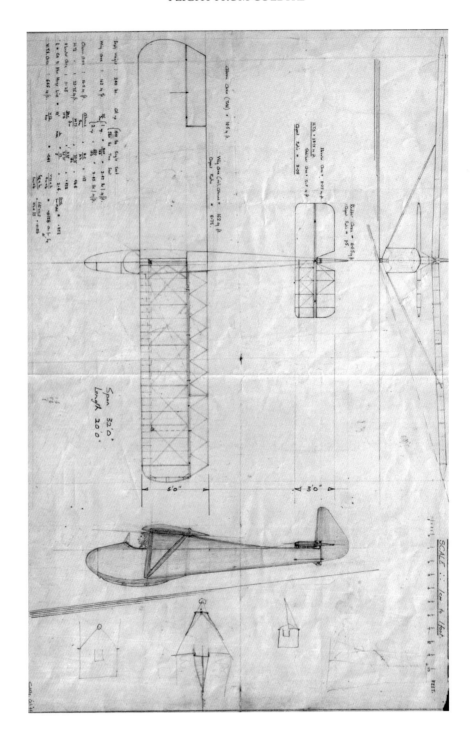

52

Obviously pretty much any project is possible with enough time to plan and money to conduct the work, but I had no idea how much funding, or time, would be available, so I had to approach this with as open a mind as possible. Being a concept not previously considered by the authorities as something the general populous would look to do in their spare time, my first major stumbling block was going to be finding a way to make it legal. One cannot simply build a flying machine and launch it into the air. All manner of laws come into play when one takes to the skies.

I have always understood that legislation is pretty clear and succinct – you either can do something or you can't – a theory possibly only confused by some local variations as to what rule falls into which category. When I was professionally studying aviation legislation, I was delighted that it seemed this situation existed here too, manifesting itself in either the 'Book of Can' or the 'Book of Can't' with countries adapting the one (and only one) they desired the most. In the UK, we all abide by the 'Book of Can' – essentially if it is written down as a rule that you can do it – you go for it. This is great for the conventional, but in a time with litigation action increasing, health and safety policy making on the rise, and the ability to choose to accept or not the repercussions of our actions being administered more and more by our politicians than us as individuals, this approach wasn't going to really work in our favour. What this does do though is protect those not directly involved with the industry, and this is why we have such an excellent aviation regulatory body in the UK, envied the world over.

As Colditz Castle geographically lies between Leipzig and Dresden in the Saxony region of Germany, the UK's Civil Aviation Authority would not have jurisdiction over our project there. Instead this would fall firmly under the control of the Luftfahrt Bundesamt (LBA), a German agency that by tradition embraces the 'Book of Can't', and for us this was an excellent development.[1]

Some calls were required, and some questions clearly needed to be asked if I was going to put my own and the company's reputation on

---

Opposite: Described as a 'General Layout', these drawings of the 'Colditz Cock' dated October 1944 are interesting in that also include information such as weights and surface areas. These are the drawings often referred to as the 'Pink Plans' due to the original colour of the paper. (Colditz Castle)

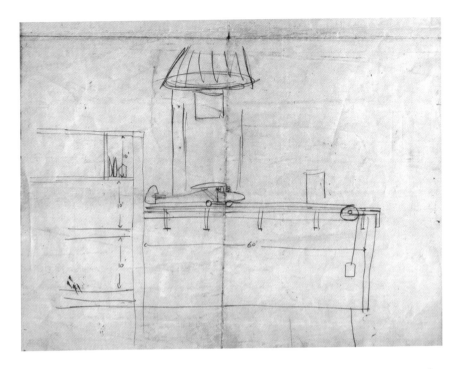

Above: Included on the rear of the October 1944 dated drawings, the 'Pink Plans', is this illustration of a proposed launching method for the 'Colditz Cock'. (Colditz Castle)

the line in front of millions of viewers. For we would only have one chance. There could be no full-scale rehearsals as the glider was likely to be damaged to a greater or lesser degree upon landing, plus we were never going to be able to take the glider apart after a trial run and carry it up to the castle roof for a second run. There simply would be no time, or money, for any second attempts. It really would be a case of all or nothing. Still, that was all in the future. For now I had to establish exactly what we were not allowed to do. I could not let the production company down on the whim of self-promotion if, at the end of the day, it was going to be legally impossible.

I knew from the start this was never going to be a manned machine, despite the production company's wishes. In my humble opinion, no job is worth risking someone's life and if we were going to do this, I was putting my foot down – nobody flies it. Yes it needed to be full size, and yes it had to be as faithful as possible to what we knew of the original, but at the end of the day this was going to be radio-controlled flight or not at all. This option certainly would give us a more flexible reception from the authorities, and I think we all considered it to be the better option to get approval, so I set about making my initial enquiries along this route.

I approached the LBA using the best of my schoolboy pigeon German, and was swiftly directed by them to their airspace policy group. The latter only wanted to know if we were going to fly anything above 500 feet or anywhere near an airport, which we weren't, so they really weren't interested and passed us back to the main LBA office. The LBA agreed with our proposal about making it a large scale model. They already had some rules about that sort of thing which would guide us, and there was some paperwork in existence which would help a great deal in the necessary applications. If we followed this route, then as long as the flying weight of our machine when ballasted did not exceed 150kg, the process for applying for and obtaining a Permit to Fly should be straightforward. With everything looking very promising, they suggested I contact the local regional LBA office in Dresden and talk with them. Having verified with the television production company that the Castle and local authorities were very much on our side, contact was made, and I was given a local representative to oversee our project should it get off the ground.

I have always believed that a well-informed production company will seek out the best people with the right skillset to get the job done, and get it done well. I was therefore quite flattered to have been considered for this roll, but I knew there were other companies in the running, so I had to advise my potential clients well and present my plans in detail. It had, however, been pointed out to me by several of my workshop customers, who had professional dealings in the television industry, that expertly planned projects, exceptional preparation and thorough testing does not a good documentary make – a programme needs drama and suspense to keep the viewers interested. I was prepared to accept that we would be kept in the dark about some things; I also knew things would change – mostly at the last minute – and I was aware that pressures would be put on us to make it interesting, but never was I actually aware how much and in how many subtle ways this would manifest itself.

The brief was complex, filled with chasm-like potholes of the unknown, and myself, my team and the presenter, Dr Hugh Hunt, had to find solutions to these problems in an entertaining and informative way. Hugh, however, had a previous record on this. A Professor of Engineering and a Fellow of Trinity College Cambridge, Dr Hunt had several years previously, and to great success, recreated Barnes Wallis' Bouncing Bomb using a length of sewer pipe and a leased DC4 flying over a Canadian lake.[2] Similarly, he had been to the former *Stalag Luft III* to demonstrate the challenges prisoners of war had faced trying to dig the 'Great Escape' through sand. All in all, a very sound chap who seemed equally unfazed by the potentially crazy escapades being planned. With an amazing ability to explain complicated engineering problems in straightforward, easy to understand language, he was the ideal man for the job.

On a personal note, Hugh's uncle had been a PoW at Colditz during the war years. This family link gave the documentary makers another angle – on the prisoners' daily life at the castle – for Hugh to explore and explain alongside his main role of tackling the launch system for the cameras. It was obvious, though, that he would need my input on launch methods, speeds and weights. With no flying experience, I would not expect him to know these things, but we would be a team and we both needed each other's help for the project to be successful. The PoWs had not finalised the exact details behind the launch method. Surviving interview records of some of those involved had explained the main points, and both the Imperial War Museum and Colditz held the 'pink plans' (or copies off) – these being the sketches penned by Bill Goldfinch of his launch proposal (more of which later), but this was all we really had to go on.

The brief stated that filming at Colditz was to be completed inside of a two week period in early 2012. This had to include set up, build, flight, and breakdown before returning to the UK, a tight timescale even if we were set at home in a warm workshop, let alone in the roof of a castle! As far as possible we had to use the same materials, same methods, and same plans, in the same location as the prisoners. A minor exception would be that we would use the Chapel's Lower Attic, whereas the prisoners had used a sectioned-off portion of the upper Chapel attic. What this did mean, however, was that we would have a little more room in which to work.

A rough guide to the PoWs' material sources was obtained from the various sources referred to in Chapter 2: wardrobes, floorboards, bed sheets, castle electrical wiring, window fittings and whatever else they could find – pretty much all of which I could buy in my local builders

Above: Dr Hugh Hunt on the Upper Terrace at Colditz Castle discussing the design of the 'Colditz Cock'. (Regina Thiede)

merchants or hardware shops. The production company wanted the necessary Permits to Fly in place before we left – a near impossible achievement that I explained from the outset was highly unlikely to happen. The glider had to be as close to the original designs as possible, for which access would be granted to various archives, and all assistance would be given to arrange the logistics of getting the completed aircraft out on to the roof. Apparently all we had to do was build the glider and provide a dummy pilot – simple?

As mentioned, exact details of the original Colditz Cock build are sketchy. We know it utilised floorboards from the theatre which were longer than the standard floorboard in Colditz. As per Bill Goldfinch's existing plans, ribs were of a built-up affair using broken up wardrobes and cupboards liberated from the castle by the inmates. Hinges were usually robbed from doors and furniture, the control cables from defunct (and sometimes not) wiring from within the castle. In order to replicate this accurately I enquired to the castle directly, confirming the floors in general were pine, about one-inch thick, and the existing relic furniture was plywood of varying thickness.

The more I looked it this, it really seemed that it was just a big model in the making. Cloth materials, as we know, were acquired by the

Opposite and above: As preparations for the final completion of the 'Colditz Cock' replica continue, and launch day approaches, Dr Hugh Hunt takes a moment to explain, for the cameras, the plans for the forthcoming flight from the castle roof. (Both Regina Thiede)

prisoners from the bed linen, stitched and then sealed with a dope-like substance made from millet. Millet seed was the basic ingredient in the prisoners' porridge ration, and it was well known that the boiling of such seed drew out the starch from within, and starch was excellent for making shirt collars stiff – so the same must be said for wing fabric.

The decision by Bill Goldfinch to use the Clark Y-H aerofoil profile was excellent for us as it offered a simple flat bottom aerofoil which would help in the build and the Computer-Aided Design (CAD) plots were readily available from a number of sources, so easy to transfer to computer.

I was intrigued by this method and wanted to work more on the millet dope. It was a complete unknown for me and I am not happy making commitments on the basis of unknowns, but armed with the research I started to formulate a rough plan. To aid build time, we would use a CAD programme to design the ribs and have them milled from plywood, slotting each unit for the two wing spars. A local Hi-Fi speaker manufacturer had machines big enough to cut these, but only to about ninety-five per cent of the wood thickness, all remaining cuts would have to be done by hand. We contacted a number of companies about getting suitable lengths of timber for longerons (thin strips of wood to which the skin of the aircraft is fastened) and spars, choosing to make these of pine, thinking that without serious laminating work, the prisoners would have probably cut down the floorboards to make these parts themselves. We were not going to have time to stitch fabric bed sheets into bags, so instead I was electing to roll out the fabric cloth and glue it to the frames before then sealing it with dope. The gingham fabric, I was finding, was only really available in forty-six-inch rolls, which wasn't going to work, but I managed to find a company in Lincolnshire that would supply rolls in seventy-two-inch lengths from abroad. We chose a slightly lighter blue than the prisoners had used, mainly as I wanted something to differentiate our replica from the previous examples.

As what I wanted to do was slightly different from that which was briefed, I decided that I would invite the researcher down to my workshop to show him or her exactly the scale of the task that the company was asking me to undertake. This I hoped would make them more accepting of the detailed proposal I was putting together for them and, maybe, might cement our dedication to their project further. The production company was shortly due to carry out a site visit to the castle, meet the local figures of authority and gather data – data I badly needed. We felt a meeting after this would help us all and so the earliest possible date post this trip was set, falling on 15 September, Battle of Britain day.

I travelled to Horsham train station to collect the researcher, and was surprised to also be introduced to Ian Duncan, the creative director and co-founder of the production company, Windfall Films. We made the gentle journey down to my workshop where, prior to their visit, I had laid out my current restoration project, a Slingsby T38, for their inspection. Being of roughly the same wingspan and built only a few years after the Second World War, the flimsy, fragile, built-up wooden structure complimented the construction of the Colditz machine beautifully. My plan failed – instead of being overwhelmed by the level of precise detail, and the hours of work and effort required to manufacture such a structure, they saw a potential flying machine, something their host for that meeting proclaimed to be potentially able to build for them in a castle attic, and their excitement grew.

Ian returned to London, whilst the researcher and I headed away for a business lunch to discuss the recent fact-finding visit to Colditz, which unfortunately turned out to be little to our benefit. All I could glean was that the former prisoner section of the castle at this point of time (2011) was mostly derelict, devoid of heating, electrical power, and in most cases floor boards. In fact, large parts of the castle were in such poor condition that access to some areas was positively dangerous and not advised, or even prohibited, by the castle's owners. Several hours into the meeting we had collated a list of 'must have' information that was absolutely essential for me to proceed. The researcher promised she would do her best and duly returned to London. Bids for the work had to be in by the end of October in the hope of securing the contract. As filming was scheduled for February, there wasn't a lot of time if this was going to happen.

Several weeks passed, many emails were exchanged, equipment was priced out, labour allocations made, and journey plans quoted. It was already the start of my busy season in the workshop, so day to day, my work concentrated on our customers, whilst special projects like this were consigned to the late evenings after our bread and butter work was complete. To complicate the situation further, we had reached the end of our lease on my tiny workshop space and I had previously made the decision to expand the company into a nearby 4,000 square foot unit, so I knew I had to relocate the entire workshop and contents ready for an opening on 1 December; I'd taken a big bite and it was all mine to chew.

I travelled up to London to make my presentation, painfully aware that it was not going to be quite what the production company had originally briefed for, but they wanted to hear me out and I was going to have my opportunity to sell my ideas hard. My proposal went very much along the following lines.

Given the fact that we had just two weeks in Colditz Castle, I proposed that we would produce a kit of parts to take to the castle, so although not involving 'prebuild' sections, we would have a basic glue-together kit of parts that would maximise our chances of pulling off a quick airframe build. Control surfaces could be made prior to leaving for Germany, and we could also get the covering of these parts just right, as controllability in the valley of the landing field was going to be paramount. I also proposed that we trial build one glider in the UK first, to assess the handling, weight and balance and glide characteristics. We would also be able to actually trial the lift-off speed of the model, and that data could be passed to Hugh Hunt to help with his launch calculations.

To say some of my proposals were met with a raised eyebrow was a bit of an understatement. However, I had to point out that a lot of issues were new and untried. For example, the millet mixture discussed by the prisoners as their preferred 'dope' was neither tested, nor its exact formula or consistency known – all this needed to be researched and tried before we left, but there wasn't provision for this in the brief. I pointed out that although working under very different conditions, sixteen prisoners in sixteen months failed to finish their glider completely, so how could four people build the same in effectively an eight day period?

For several weeks I waited to hear of any news. Then, in mid-November, the call came – we had the contract, but with some changes to my proposal. We were not to prebuild any airframe assemblies, and although the kit idea was met with approval, we were only to build one example and not the two I wanted. Likewise, there would be no pre-filming testing nor any investigation into using millet. That said, the TV company accepted our proposal to make it radio-controlled, and also that we would have to differ the original glider only in that its maximum permitted take-off weight was to be 150kg ballasted rather than the prisoners' original which was around 160kg (240lb) un-laden. There was an additional requirement to do some flying sequences to explain how a glider flies which would have to filmed before we left. Lastly, we needed to now be ready to be at Colditz, with our glider kit and all our equipment, for the first week of March 2012. That was just three months away!

Chapter 4

The Build Begins

During the previous few weeks we had been preparing for our move to our new facilities. As a result we were all set to close the old workshop around 30 November 2011 and open on 1 December in the new site about one mile away. Our maintenance work in the workshop was already in full swing, and as I had business interests in the Czech Republic at the time, I still had a 2,000 mile round trip to do before the end of November, little could be done right away except order the wood and fabric material and wait for the dust to settle.

December arrived, and with the new workshop up and running on our local village airstrip, attention could be given to our Colditz work. We had the drawings now from the Imperial War Museum (IWM) and the castle's archives, and an initial sketch was prepared to examine just how things would best be assembled. The design showed a typical box-section fuselage with frames spaced roughly evenly down the structure. Wing ribs we knew were going to simply slide down the spars, and would be braced internally with more square section material. As per the original design, we would top hinge the control surfaces using steel door hinges and, therefore, the same rib structure could be used to make the aileron sections rather than designing alternatives. Happily the rear wing spar was going to act as a handy anchor point for these, so the wings themselves could be built light and quickly.

One of my colleagues offered to convert the original Colditz drawings into a CAD version for cutting, scaling straight from the wartime plans. Minor inaccuracies in these drawings were ironed out, such as the frame widths and spacings, allowing the fuselage to taper nicely rather than meander in and out as might otherwise be the case.

Our drawings were finalised over Christmas and taken to the locally-based Hi-Fi speaker manufacturer who plotted our points, checked them, and through some magical engineering planning software, managed to squeeze all the parts we needed onto five super large sheets of plywood.

Here, however, I have to make a confession in that we had decided to go against the wishes of the programme makers. I totally understood the need for raw experiences and of discovering things as we went along. Nevertheless, they also wanted us to deliver on our word, and they wanted a permit in place to allow us to fly. I had given them my advice, but it had not been taken on board. I was determined not to let them down, so I made the decision there and then I was going to build two kits. Having spent the majority of December in discussion with the Saxony office of the LBA and the German Large Scale Model Association, it was deemed the best way to ensure regulatory compliance was to start a production line. Large scale model testing is not intended to be carried out above a town, in fact the requirements are very restricted. However, it became apparent that one could carry out tests on a model and then, if fit for purpose, a second machine could be built and flown without restrictions other than those dictated by the rules of the air.

The direction I had to take was therefore straightforward. We would make two kits as per my original plan. One would in fact be for testing, a process which would also give us valuable practice in terms of the build, ascertain how long it would take to build which bits, and allow us to make modifications along the way which could be incorporated into the second unbuilt kit. Testing could then begin on the prototype, and the results of this could be sent to the German authorities for approval. Essentially then, the suitability of our machine for the flight could be agreed with the Germans before we arrived and, subject to an authorities' visit to assess the quality of the build for its designated purpose, the vital permit permissions should be easily obtained. Documents were downloaded, fees paid and two Colditz gliders were duly registered in Germany.

We gave the go ahead for two sets of ribs, and two sets of fuselage frames to be made and, in mid-January 2012, I took the company 4x4 to collect our parts from the speaker factory. To my surprise, there was not much to see at all! Wrapped in plastic and bound up for transport, all the timber for two machines took up about half a roof-rack and, when

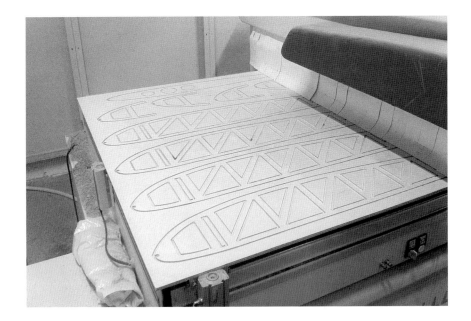

Above: Using technology not available to the prisoners at Colditz, here the ribs for both of our replicas are being cut from a single sheet of ply on a computer numerical control machine. (Author)

Opposite: The first steps are taken in the laying out and construction of the rear fuselage for the first of our replicas. Note the other parts that can be seen laid out on the workshop floor. (Author)

---

placed on the floor, considering all the time and effort that had gone into it to date, the results looked pitiful. Did the prisoners at Colditz really expect to fly from the castle in such a flimsy craft?

I needed to assemble a good reliable build team for our time at Colditz, and what a team I had. Initially I obtained the services of Malcolm Blows, an airline pilot by profession, but an avid modeller by hobby. He started by advising me on the issues with radio-controlled models of that size, and the equipment in use today for flying them. I dearly hoped Malcom would be able to join us, but knew getting time from his work schedule was going to be difficult. Jess Nyahoe was next in the team. Working for me already, Jess had shown to be a keen and

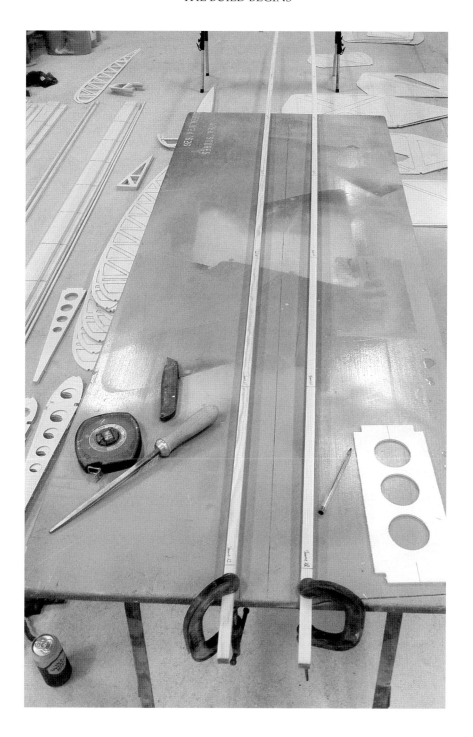

committed worker on our customers' aircraft, always popular with them her personality shone through and always kept us laughing and in good spirits. Keen on the historical aspect of the project, she threw herself completely at the enterprise, and her work on the project was significant and unfortunately, slightly overlooked in the completed documentary. My good friend Ben Watkins joined us as the third member of the party. A glider pilot and long-time employee of the aviation industry, Ben offered his services pretty much every evening for months, both in the workshop and for the brainstorming sessions. Regularly turning up most evenings, not only with dinner on nearly every occasion but often bringing his interested work colleagues with him (who were quickly tasked with lending a hand), Ben could always be counted on to provide an alternative viewpoint on many of the technical issues we encountered. If at times we felt overwhelmed with problems and deadlines, Ben was the one who reminded me that the early hours of the morning were certainly the time to go home.

I knew we had to save on time, and time we had in the UK but not in the castle. As a keen plastic model kit builder, I was happy with following a 'big model' principle of assembly and duplicated my methods across both kits. Plans were referenced and the rib locations were plotted on the wing spars. Several flaws were discovered in the wood, similar I imagine to the issues the PoWs would have encountered during the same process, so I quickly selected out prototype stock, and film flight stock, leaving the best quality spar and longeron material for the final flyer. Longerons, it may be recalled, are thin strips of material to which the skin of the aircraft is fastened. Plotting the ribs accurately and square would save us time in the castle, and we pre-cut the spar lengths exactly, weighing spar pairs to get as close as possible to equal weights for each wing. This turned out to be a lucky move as we were to later find out on our first day at Colditz.

With wing ribs batched into prototype and film flyer sets, we then began trimming the stock intended for the prototype. Fairly quickly a design flaw on our CAD plans became apparent. This was that we hadn't fully allowed for the rear spar recess and, as a result, every single one of our ribs would need adjusting by hand to fit. With a busy maintenance season in full swing, Colditz work was still relegated to the evenings after normal working hours, and the laborious job of preparing every rib by hand began. After the first week, we had enough altered ribs to attempt the first wing construction and I am pleased to think the planning we had put in to date paid off here.

With no workshop heating, we could replicate the conditions we expected to encounter in the castle's attic and therefore we could accurately assess the suitability of the expanding epoxy glue products we intended to use in a similar fashion to the way the prisoners would have made the original. By sliding the ribs in place and gluing each one securely to the forward spar we could quickly assemble a wing panel with reasonable accuracy in about three hours between two people. The tricky insertions of the D-box half ribs and leading edge pieces did not do much for the rigidity, but when we set Rib 1 square with cross and drag braces, the strength of the wing became suddenly apparent. Within a full working day, we had one basic wing panel, short of an aileron and its tip brace, but the majority of it was there and could come off the build trestles.

Notes were made and some experiments regarding the number of braces required versus the increasing weight were undertaken before we settled on the exact total needed. Duplicates of these were also manufactured for the flight kit. Production of the second wing naturally progressed faster, and by the end of the second build day we had two wings and had expanded our flight kit to include all the extra bits we knew we were going to need. We were averaging 12kg per wing panel uncovered and un-wired, which I was happy with. I needed to save weight on the tail to minimise the ballast requirement, but it was becoming obvious from our experience with the thin wing ribs that the fuselage was going to end up needing a lot of reinforcement.

Fuselage construction was carried out next. From the outset I elected to double up the main load frames with a light sandwich material in the middle to give strength. It is to these frames (also called formers) that load-bearing longerons are attached which run in the longitudinal direction of the aircraft.

The wing mountings to Frame 3 and Frame 5 were selected for the first treatments. The frames themselves needed gluing and clamping under considerable even load to stay properly bonded, and it took nearly a day to prepare all the frames so that they were ready to go. Not knowing if this was going to be effective, we elected not to modify the film kit just yet until we had test-flown the prototype, so we went full steam ahead to get the fuselage done. Steam, as it happened, was going to be an issue. From the wartime plans, it was obvious that the main

Above: The first fuselage nearing completion. The longerons have been steamed into place, but the excess material still needs to be trimmed off. (Author)

Below: The completed port wing of the first replica is shown here awaiting the application of the fabric skin. (Author)

longitudinal datum was the top longeron, and by design to keep this flat was not going to be as straightforward as expected.

All the other parts of the Colditz Glider sloped and curved beautifully so I decided we would only need to construct a short build table, long enough to support only the rear section of fuselage. We would construct the main portions upside down. I had a collapsible bench table that was pretty much near flat in all directions and, after plotting out the longeron and rib positions on the table, construction began at the fin post.

Despite marking centre lines on all the frames and tacking the longerons to the bench whilst the glue set, the rear fuselage sprang up during one working evening. Keen to move on, I somewhat hurriedly, and as it proved prematurely, lifted the fuselage to test for rigidity and it rapidly began to fall apart under the weight of the lower (in this case on top) longeron. A quick return to the build table was required. After re-tacking the top longerons to the bench and a hasty attack with the metal setsquare and a considerable number of cross braces, I departed the workshop in the early hours for home and some well-earned rest.

We were getting close to the end of January now, and although we knew where we were with the wings, the fuselage construction was proving more complicated than expected. It was a continuous battle between adding strength but not to the detriment of the all-up weight. The lack of structure in the rear fuselage was causing the whole thing to twist every time it was moved from the bench. Gusset pieces were added as per the original drawings and only when we had done this around the complete rear fuselage box section, did it begin to hold shape. With so much weight, we were going to have to make the tail as light as possible, but that was going to be for another day.

Following a major push on our customer winter maintenance work, I switched from these tasks to work full time on the Colditz project. With just a month to run until we were expected to leave, there was still a vast amount of work to be done, and I was starting to doubt whether we could achieve it.

Armed with a vat of coffee, I spent another day duplicating these gusset pieces before we could finally move on to the complicated bit. The positioning of Frame 3 and Frame 5 was going to be critical if we were to get the wing incidence right. However, with our CAD cut-out frame we had caused a headache by building it upside down. Allowing the longerons to overhang by the minimum that we possibly could, we manufactured trestles to sit between the frames of the same height as the table. By gluing only the upper longeron to the frame, we could brace these sections square with gussets to hold their position before attempting to bend the lower longerons into position. Ideally, we would be steaming these sections of longerons in a pipe, but it was unlikely the prisoners would have had such a commodity and it was equally unlikely we would have access to anything like that ourselves. They would probably have had access to a stove, and by boiling water and soaking the wood, they probably would have been able to bend these sections over a period of time. We attempted the same with the workshop kettle and by hanging bigger and heavier tools from the extreme end of the longeron, over about twelve hours we achieved the same effect.

For the last two frames, which needed to bend down to meet the bottom longeron, we decided to repeat the process. Using heavy duty string, we noosed each longeron and through an elaborate entanglement of knots and threading we could slowly pull all four longerons together with each wetting with boiling water. It took a whole day, but it worked.

Returning to the workshop the following morning we discovered that it did not appear to have fallen out of shape and that the glue had held, even though it was obvious it was under extreme load. Studying the plans, it seemed the original glider had an element of ply skinning applied to the front cockpit area, and this I knew would help us not only by holding the front square, but also it would share some of the load from the longerons to the skin. Our spare ply was quickly glued and tacked from Frame 1 to Frame 3 and instantly it looked like we had a fuselage. For the first time we could safely turn over the fuselage and glue the top coaming in place – and what a magnificent sight it was!

We knew we had to launch this machine pretty rapidly, and it being made up from big subsections we had a lot of different bolt-together masses to move around quickly. Basic engineering principles dictate that you try and tie all these masses together, and I wanted to tie everything together with triangles to make this work. The wing struts would naturally brace the wings to the top and bottom of Frame 3. If I could tie from 5 into Frame 3 as well, our wing structure should be sound and not feel inclined to twist off its mountings upon acceleration. We would be accelerating the aircraft off a nose-hook mounted at the base of Frame 1, so it was decided to install a keel beam to hold everything together.

Top: Work underway on the tail mounting. With no information on the tail mounting of the original 'Colditz Cock' available to us, the design of this part of our replica was completed in-house. (Author)

Above: Filming underway at the Cambridge Gliding Club during February 2012. (Author)

The plans showed a keel skid, very similar to glider designs of the time, generally sprung; we couldn't see that for the one-off trip, the prisoners would have designed in such a luxury, so neither did we. From the plans we could also see that the upper sections of frames 1 to 5 were all in a level plain, so this naturally became the top of our keel and essentially probably the base for the seats for the two 'crew'. Using the same pine material as the wing spars, we could box in this lower front section, increasing the weight forward of the centre of gravity and therefore reducing the overall weight required for ballasting (I hoped).

There were no specific drawings for the hook assembly the prisoners intended to use, so working back through the designs of the day, I settled on a hook similar to the bungee hook of the 1930s. Before the war, gliding was becoming very popular in the UK. This mostly took the form of clubs that gathered on a local hill and launched their gliders from the top by pulling on two bungee ropes, allowing the glider to sail majestically from the top of the slope and glide gracefully to the bottom. Post-war, this method of launching was still to be used by the Air Training Corps for 'ground hopping' Slingsby T38 'Grasshopper' aircraft, a type I had three wrecks of in my workshop at the time.

It was straightforward, therefore, to copy the setting angles of this hook and actually use one of the examples in our Colditz glider. The hook, by design, allows a good pull on the aircraft bolted to it, but as the rope becomes slack, the ring on the end of the launching rope falls off the back of the hook, allowing the glider to disconnect freely – something we wanted to be assured of when we believed we were to tie it to a bathtub and drop it off a building!

We were aware that Bill Goldfinch had mentioned using manpower rather than a tub of concrete, but an interview he had recorded, and which was mentioned earlier, only came to light when I was writing this book. Until then we assumed that Pat Reid's bathtub method was ultimately the one chosen by the prisoners. So that was what we had initially worked to. Whether we would have actually found ten or fifteen volunteers to jump down the bell tower is also questionable!

Another consideration was that we were going to hang the bathtub from the glider, this being the only safe way to release all the stored energy in the system. To suddenly release the bathtub cleanly could 'jerk' the glider, peaking a load and causing damage to the delicate structure. If we were to restrain the glider, the load could slowly be taken from the bathtub through the rope, taking out all of the slack, so that when we let the glider go, it would accelerate cleanly. With calculations by the prisoners looking at one ton of weight in a bathtub, and with the LBA placing limitations on us of 150kg maximum, this needed to be one strong glider.

Although not a 'product' available to the prisoners, we were already using tie bars extensively for strut fittings and wing fittings; we knew they got their hands on door hinges and window bars which were similar in dimensions, just that they had less holes. I decided it was probably in our interest to bolt the hook to a length of tie bar that would also be bolted to the keel beam and would, at the opposite end, be bolted to the carry-through tie bar that took the lower lift strut mounts. With this achieved, we knew we could pull all the loads through the keel beam, with metalwork bolted to the wing strut attachment points which in turn meant all the heavy items should follow the hook and, hopefully, the lighter airframe around it would follow too. Only tests would tell.

However, time for any testing was going to be tight. We were now into the first week of February 2012, and there was only three weeks to go and all we had was a basic airframe. The issue was suddenly complicated by a spontaneous piece of filming being required. The production company was due to visit Hugh at Trinity College Cambridge to break the news to him on camera as to what our project was going to be. To keep things 'raw' I didn't realise that Hugh had only been informed of his need to host a show and actually didn't know completely the subject matter, only that it would involve Colditz Castle. He was to be introduced to the subject on camera and his initial thoughts recorded. The following day, he would meet me for the first time and I would take him flying in a glider so he, and the audience, could get a basic understanding of the principles of flight. It would also help with a bit of promotion for the British Gliding Association and the sport in general.

With flying scheduled for an unbelievably tight date of 16 February, I had a lot to organise. Not the least of these was to regain my flying instructors' rating. This had lapsed in 2007. This was when I had a busy job in the airlines, and a recently purchased cottage in need of complete renovation at the time put paid to my commitments to instructing.

I spoke with the chairman of the Cambridge Gliding club at Gransden Lodge airfield. This was a place I had previously resided at in 2002 and so, having also completed a few evenings of instruction there, I was familiar with the airfield, its operation and the surroundings. A deal was struck to use the facilities and the cleanest, youngest two-seater on their fleet was selected for the task. I also rang my good friends and customers at the Surrey Hills Gliding Club at Kenley. I already looked after their entire club fleet and the vast majority of the private owners there, and I badly needed some recurrent instructor training to get back in the swing of things. The Chief Flying Instructor kindly offered his services and I shot up on the Tuesday before filming to spend the day winching. Three launches, and two emergency launch failures later, I was back on the ground and feeling pretty up to date.

As I was paying up, the phone rang; it was the Chairman of the Cambridge Club. He informed me that after checking their insurance I couldn't fly on just the sign-off from one of their instructors. I was compelled to have a refresher course from the regional examiner – who, luckily, just happened to be based at the club. Only after this would I be good to go.

Lucky for me, that week also saw Pat Willis, an individual who would become a stalwart of the project, join the team. Until this point I had been relying on my good friend Malcolm Blows to provide me with guidance on the more modern radio-control equipment. It had been decades since I had last been involved with the hobby at the White Horse Model Club in Oxfordshire – and lots had changed in that time. I had really hoped that Malcolm was going to be able to join us for the project, but unfortunately, mid-project, we discovered his daytime commitments to flying passengers around for a UK airline was going to prohibit the trip. Malcolm brought Pat in though, and I am forever grateful that we made his acquaintance. Pat had unfortunately just been put out of work and was looking out for a new venture. Flying model planes is more than a hobby to Pat, it is his passion and his knowledge of the subject is immense. Malcolm brought him in just before I was due to go flying at Kenley so our meeting was hurried. I explained a few of the problems I was up against, what we needed to do with the job, and what problems we were having. He knew of a few solutions off the top of his head, and clearly knowing what needed doing, he was duly hired in a matter of minutes.

With Pat on board I could leave him to the electrical side of things. It also meant that we had a 'pilot' and final forth member of our team for the mission ahead. Pat had some large model flying experience, but

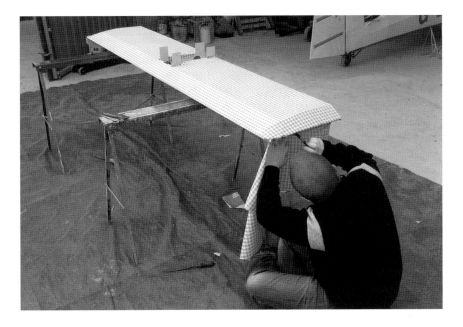

Above: The fabric skin is applied to the tail of our first replica. (Author)

Below: The fuselage of the test replica receives its fabric covering. (Author)

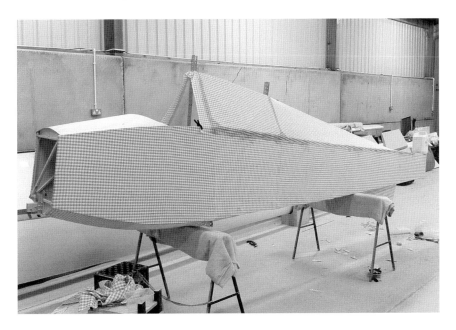

nothing ever this big. At ten metres the model is actually amongst the largest ever built, and few in the UK have experience of flying models of this scale, but I had every faith in Pat and seeing some of the models he had in his collection, I knew he could handle it. The next day he came in clutching a purchase list of equipment. He already had a top-end radio transmitter which he kindly offered to use in the project, but the servo and receiver gear all had to be purchased. For safety, we doubled up on everything, with super huge metal gear servos that could actually drive each control surface individually if the main servo failed. These primary and slave servo systems were made into servo packs, each with a dedicated receiver and power supply and were mounted at each control surface to minimise losses through extensive wiring. Pat set up a test rig in the workshop which ran each servo through its full extent for several hours each. Brand new servos we knew were bench tested, but we wanted to make doubly sure they were good for the job so we tested them again – losing a unit on the roof of the castle was not going to be a good outcome and therefore was not an option.

I made my way up to Cambridge Gliding Club for my glider examination very early in the morning; the weather forecast was unseasonably good and we were expecting clear skies by mid-morning. This was perfect, allowing me time to carry out all my checks.

Arriving at the same time as the duty crew, I pulled out their newest ASK 21, and carried out the daily inspection.[1] A quick wash and a clean and she looked lovely – it was then time for briefings and to meet the examiner. Briefings done, we took the machine out to the launch point, up the wire, a few exercises and we were back pretty quickly. Expecting another trip, I rolled up to the launch point as briefed, but out hopped the instructor who wanted to debrief. All done, one flight. Maybe I hadn't forgotten too much?

Coffee was duly supped and it was then I saw a car making its way around the airfield. In it was Tom, the Editor, who I was yet to meet, and Jason, the Production Manager. Introductions over, I discovered this was the advance party here to set up cameras and microphones for the filming. Hugh would follow shortly, and I wasn't to meet him until the cameras were rolling.

Internal cameras, external cameras, radio mics, battery packs, all had to be squeezed in and checked for non-interference. After a couple of sound checks we were ready for the off. As Hugh was an Australian it was necessary, of course, to await the announcement of the cricket scores on the radio before any flying got under way. I instantly found him a most humble and inquiring chap and I liked him. He understood as much as I did that the job that lay before us was massive. Hugh, though, had only just been handed his task, whereas I'd been working for nearly three months already – he had just a matter of weeks to complete his task.

We talked for a while before the camera operators went off for the strap-in and safety briefing. Again, after relaying once more about the canopy jettison and what to do in a bale out, we set off for the first of many flights. I picked winch launching for the demonstration as it accurately depicted the initial acceleration we required for launching at Colditz, and also meant in the short daylight hours we could get multiple flights in should camera failure occur.

With three launches in the bag, the camera crew jumped in the tug, and we took an aero-tow to 4,000 feet in the late afternoon sun for some air-to-air footage. Hugh also tried his hand at a bit of gliding. Rolling up next to the hangar as we really were the only flyers of the day, I reflected that it had gone well, although Hugh now had an awful lot of questions. I helped pack the glider away in the hangar as quickly as possible to let the Cambridge Club guys go. Thanking them, we retired to the bar to discuss the project in more depth. With the camera set up in the corner, we sat for over an hour discussing various technical aspects and the problems and pitfalls that we knew we had to overcome. With the camera crew looking on frustratingly (our conversation was getting quite technical), we had to call it quits for the day. I hadn't let on to Hugh at the time that we were building a test machine, but we swapped phone numbers and addresses and agreed to talk in the near future.

Setting off back to Sussex I mulled over the fact that it had been a long but productive day, though I knew there was going to be no rest yet. Our time to the journey to Saxony could be measured in days, and the parts for the replica Colditz Cock were still a long way from completion.

When I returned to the workshop, it was apparent that the model was becoming alarmingly heavy. The LBA wanted an update on progress and we were going to have to do some serious weight saving if it was going to fly. The general rule of thumb for aeroplanes and models alike is that for every unit mass of weight you add to the tail of a conventional flying machine like ours, you have to add four times that at the nose to get it to balance. We had added considerable weight at the nose for the box keel beam, but tail lightness was now the next task to be considered, and light it was really going to have to be.

We had the rib profiles already cut, and I decided the lightest way forward was going to be a hollow forward spar arrangement, hollow in that I would only fit a top and bottom boom to the ribs, and a thinner solid rear spar to take the hinges and bending loads of the elevator. Building flat on a bench proved easy, and with the first ribs cut and glued square, it proved to be a fairly fast task, completed in one good evening of work. The elevator itself was made in one piece, top hinged and with the servo drives mounted close inboard. Using standard door hinges, the whole thing weighed in at around 1.8kg and I was very happy.

The rudder, unfortunately, proved trickier. I have always wondered about the rudder on this machine. It was neither efficient nor straightforward to make; all in all, it was possibly about the worst shape you would want for a glider. Gliders inherently suffer badly from adverse yaw issues and as such have large surface area rudders, particularly in the older designs. Now the Colditz glider proportionally wasn't one with particularly significant aspect ratio, but what it did have was massive ailerons, in the region of half the wing span in total. This by design would create massive adverse yaw and, with a fairly slender, tapering rear fuselage, would require some rudder work to make it fly properly. The rudder in Bill Goldfinch's design wasn't going to offer any of this. With such a big wing, the turbulated air from the back of the wing would mix with the air pushed out of the way by the boxy fuselage meaning that the vast majority of the rudder would be masked by the disturbed air from the profile of all of the machine in front of it. The only possible clear air would be found towards the top

---

Opposite top: A dummy pilot tries out the first replica for size. (Author)

Opposite bottom: A big moment for the replica build team. Here the first of our two replicas is about to be tested as part of the process for obtaining its Luftfahrt-Bundesamt (LBA) approval on 2 March 2012. The LBA is the German equivalent of the British Civil Aviation Authority. This testing took place at Partridge Green in West Sussex. (Author)

Above: A resplendent Colditz Castle complete with the new runway fitted high up on the roof of the attic above the former French quarters. (Ben Watkins)

Above: At last the assembly is complete and the glider is ready for its ground-breaking flight. (Regina Thiede)

Below: As the big moment approaches, 'Alex' looks out from the cockpit of the glider over the town of Colditz. (Ben Watkins)

Above: Barely visible to anyone in the inner courtyard at Colditz (what was the prisoners' courtyard), only a wing tip of the glider can be seen to the left of the chapel tower. (Author)

Above: Looking down on the intended landing site from over the rear of the glider's fuselage. (Ben Watkins)

Below: The finished glider sits proudly on the runway awaiting its moment to take to the air for the first time. (Ben Watkins)

Top: Airborne! After all the planning and effort of the previous weeks and months, the new Colditz Cock is launched from the roof of Colditz Castle and heads out over the town below. (Windfall Films)

Middle: Seconds after lift-off, one of the various cameras mounted on the glider captures this view of some of the buildings between Colditz Castle and the River Mulde. (Windfall Films)

Bottom: This snapshot from the film footage taken from the castle roof shows how far the glider dropped after leaving the runway – it can be seen to the left of the runway having got as far as the river. (Windfall Films)

Top: This onboard camera shows the view that 'Alex' enjoyed as the glider crossed the River Mulde and closed in on the landing ground. (Windfall Films)

Middle: Seen from the landing ground, the glider gracefully continues its descent from the runway, which already seems some distance off. (Windfall Films)

Bottom: The glider undertakes a banking turn to continue its final run in to the landing ground. (Windfall Films)

Top: The last few seconds of flight for 'Alex' and the latest version of the Colditz Cock. (Windfall Films)

Middle: The camera mounted on the nose of the glider captures the moment of impact on the landing site beside the River Mulde. (Windfall Films)

Bottom: Seen from a different angle, here the glider is banking around prior to touching down. (Windfall Films)

Above: The exact spot where the glider touched down after its remarkable flight. (Ben Watkins)

of the rudder, in this case the smallest area part, so its usefulness was likely to be minimal. The possible range of movements was recorded on the wartime drawings, and it was clear that we were going to need all of this. I didn't want to deviate from the original design, and considering there was no fixed fin as such on the original design, all of the yawing forces were going to be transmitted through the rudder – it needed to be strong, but it also needed to be so light.

I decided upon a similar boom spar to the elevator for the rudder, boxed in properly in the lower section to give as much strength to the structure as possible. The leading edge was finished with a dowel rod and the curved trailing edge was made up with a steamed three-ply laminate. Hinges in this instance were simple triangle blocks of ply bolted through the middle. A more permanent design was considered, but what had to be borne in mind was the circumstances in which the glider would be put together. It was all very well building a glider in our Sussex workshop, and though it would be a laborious job replicating another in the attic loft of Colditz, this would be fairly simple. That, though, was only part of the operation. We were going to have to take this out of a hole in the roof, past a clock tower and then assemble it on a narrow roof runway high up the side of a castle. We needed a simple, sure-fire way to assemble and disassemble this flying machine in a very unnatural environment and it was going to have to work.

With the tail-feathers complete, the ailerons were constructed in a similar fashion to the elevator, but with the control pushrods mounted at the mid-hinge point. Again, top-hinged, these large ailerons were heavy, and required two of our biggest metal gear servos to move them. Nevertheless, it was the last week of February and what we appeared to have was a complete glider.

Thoughts now turned to covering the wings and fuselage. I was worried by the whole idea of using millet. Being used to conventional cellulose nitrate and butyrate-based products, introducing a new material was something that concerned me. Originally the prisoners stitched the fabric to the airframe, and then doped the millet onto the fabric to seal it. We certainly weren't going to have time to stitch the fabric, so I elected to glue the fabric with fabric cement to the wooden structure, and I really wanted to use dope to seal it.

Ben and I elected for an early start on the Saturday, and with the weather unseasonably glorious, the rudder was selected for the first coverings. Glue applied, it dried quickly on the apron in front of the workshop and with some thinners to hand we quickly covered the rudder with the gingham cotton. A few liberal coats of cellulose dope were applied and within an hour we had a covered surface. The tailplane and elevators followed, each component being weighed, and more dope applied until it seemed airtight. On the Sunday we covered both wings in one long day, but wanting to save on weight we only doped the lower surface, hoping to at least get a 'parachute' effect for the flight test, without adding too much weight doping the whole structure.

By Monday, we were ready to cover the fuselage. With some control cable locked in as the fuselage spine, we made a final inspection inside before we rolled out the fabric. Instantly, the structure we had poured over for many weeks became a fuselage, and we could see the machine forming in front of our eyes. By the early hours of the morning, we had glued, covered and trimmed the entire fuselage and we stood back to admire our work. There she sat, pristine, waiting to fly, a complete little glider, so familiar in shape after months of work, but sitting on the workshop floor, built from scratch. I was getting quite emotional.

What we needed now was an 'escapee'. Despite the fact that the glider would be unmanned, it still had to look the part, and so it needed an authentic-looking pilot. So the next question to be answered was where to get one? I discounted using an entire manikin, the weight was not something we could afford. Searching the internet, I found some very lightweight male torsos for a reasonable price, and, with further searching, I located a bag of Styrofoam heads – perfect! The following day, the items arrived. A quick trim of the foam heads with a saw gave us a relatively proportioned neck, and with a copious application of Gripfill adhesive, the two were bonded together and our 'pilot' born. Jess' artistic talent was sought to make our dummy as life-like as possible, and she retired to the warmth of the workshop office with her paint box to get started. It was hours later that I turned around and was completely taken unawares by what greeted my eyes. Jess had completed her work, and lacking any other clothing, had dressed the manikin with her hoodie. From even a short distance, it was pretty convincing to all that somebody else was in the room, and I think we were all rather startled in the tired states we found ourselves in.

The following morning, a trip to the local charity shop secured his 'escape kit', consisting of a grey wool jumper and a flat cap. Proportionally, we hadn't quite got his neck correct, so a thin black turtle

Above: The moment of truth approaches during the LBA testing with the replica about to make its first 'hop' into the air. (Author)

Below: With one successful 'hop' completed, during which the nose detached itself on landing, the glider is prepared for another trial 'hop'. Again successful, two days later the team departed for Colditz Castle. (Author)

neck jumper was acquired to hide this minor imperfection in his physique, and it certainly looked the part. As his fate was still unknown, and as the original PoW team had intended to decide the two occupants on the night of the launch, we felt it was improper to name the pilot after any particular individual. It had been pointed out that the features and hairstyle of our pilot closely resembled Jess' brother Alex, and so duly noted, we settled on 'Alex' for our 'PoW' – the fifth and final member of the team!

There was now just a week to go and we still needed to make lift struts, manufacture a nose bowl, balance the machine with lead, install the power packs and servo gear, and then set up the controls and conduct the test flight. In addition we had to load up the flight kit, tools, equipment and clothes.

The production team held a conference call on the Monday. This included Hugh and key production team members and allowed me to talk for the first time to the carpenters and rope access team. We all exchanged updates, with the production team being particularly keen to know where we stood on a permit. I had to reiterate again that we were not going to get this in place before we left for Germany, but that I had done all we could up to this point and that a meeting was set for the end of the first week at Colditz with the authorities. This was met with much discussion, the team understandably concerned that we would be mobilising a large number of people not knowing if we could actually fly.

I knew that I had everything in place to secure the permit, but that we had to test our prototype first before gaining approval, and then our second machine would just need an inspection for quality on site – I wished that I could reassure them, but I couldn't. I said we were ready to pack, our flight kit was all prepared and that if they needed any other equipment to be carried, they should just let me know. Happy that my part was done, I sat back and listened to the rest of the conference call putting in thoughts occasionally as required. As we finished up the Editor said he'd like to visit our workshop and would tomorrow be ok? 'Oh dear', I thought, as I peered from the office door into the workshop, full of Colditz glider and bins full of masses of cut gingham fabric. 'Sure,' I said, 'I'll pick you up at the train station'.

Well, it was a long night that night, clearing all traces of our work on the prototype to date, and sorting our flight kit into sections on the floor for inspection, but making it look considerably big enough to justify all the hours of working to date – but what to do with what we had built? I had nowhere else to store the glider, and the workshop was full with customer machines. In the early evening I had it figured, we had a customer aircraft in for painting, if I could paint it this evening, it could come out in the morning and I could load the Colditz prototype into the booth and close it up – marvellous, all I had to do was paint an entire aircraft overnight. In the early hours of the morning, my painting was done, the heaters were on and I crawled into bed at home, knowing that it was only a few hours until I needed to be back to move everything around.

With the Editor on the train and expected by mid-morning, bleary-eyed I returned to work. Pat and I rolled the freshly painted machine from the booth and after a clean down, and with minutes to go until I needed to leave, we loaded the Colditz glider in and locked it all down. It was frustrating to think that we were losing time just as we were so close to finishing the job.

Leaving Pat to make some wing struts, I set off to pick up Tom from Horsham train station and bring him to the workshop. I had decided that I wasn't going to leave things to chance, with so much to risk in the castle. If we dropped a control surface, or even damaged it getting it onto the roof, the flight and the film could be lost. I therefore decided to own up to prebuilding some items, so along with the flight kit for Germany, I had placed the rudder and ailerons from the prototype out for him to see as well.

When we arrived, I explained that although I fully intended building a whole glider in the attic in Colditz, in case we damaged something on the morning of the flight I had prebuilt some 'spares' of the lighter, more fragile components, that I wanted to take with us. He accepted this as wise, and seemed happy that we had a whole kit ready to go. Coffees imbibed, and introductions made to Pat and Jess, who he hadn't yet met, I escorted him from the workshop, giving the team the nod as I closed the door to continue as previously briefed.

Tom the Editor was happy; he had been worried that we had fallen behind, and wanted to make sure all was in order. They were, after all, committing a considerable amount of money to the project and we were still at that time an unknown quantity. I wanted to tell him all the work and effort we had put in to the project so far, but we were so close, and he was happy, so why spoil things! I dropped him back at the station, wished him well, and rushed back to the workshop as quickly as I could.

By the time that I got back Pat already had the power packs and servo units in position. Control throws were being completed and we were getting close. I pulled in my biggest spare glider trailer and jacked it for inspection. I left Pat working the electrical systems whilst the trailer had a complete service, wheels, axle, hitch and lights. Beginning to load our tools and equipment, I realised quite how much stuff we actually needed. With a build bench on the floor, wing trestles, cutting tools, and the kit itself, although it didn't weigh too much, it was extremely bulky, and we still had our personal bags to pack. As I calculated our route and the likely difficulties which we might face in the journey ahead, Tom, now back in London, called to say he wanted to send some lighting equipment and camera kit for us to take with us – no problem I said, courier it on down.

Due to leave on the coming Sunday, on the Wednesday we made two nose bowls. The prisoners had used papier-mâché, but with the weather forecast as it was for Germany, we thought we were very likely to get wet, and I didn't want to see the front of our machine sagging and gaining yet more weight on the launch run, with the likelihood of depositing remnants of the nose on to the unsuspecting town inhabitants below. I decided fibre glass was the way to go. With Jess carving up a mould from insulation foam, we quickly laid up two epoxy resin and cloth nose bowls and when cured, doped gingham fabric to the front.

That afternoon we rigged the wings and spent some time setting up angles and washout, which is the reduction of the angle of the wing towards the tip to improve its flying characteristics. The original incidence was 1.5 degrees and we kept with this as per the plan. The actual total washout wasn't clear from the plans, so we played safe and reduced the tip washout to zero degrees. A phone call from London told me the equipment we were to carry to Germany was on its way by courier, and that we could expect it that evening.

I needed to be home to pack, so headed off. Arriving back in the morning, I opened the door and was horrified at the sight that greeted me. The pile of equipment was vast, and most of it heavy-looking. A quick phone call with the Production Manager confirmed this was what they wanted – but there was no way we could carry all that stuff. It was clear that the TV team clearly did not appreciate how much material we were capable of carrying. I could not take all they had sent down so I decided to help as much as I could by selecting the bulky items and the fragile stuff. Nevertheless, despite this pairing down it was soon becoming obvious that we were getting close to the maximum trailer weight.

After much shuffling, I got about half of the stuff in, and that was the most I was prepared to take. I phoned London back, explained the situation and they agreed to have the remainder collected that night by courier. Otherwise, as far as the glider went, with 2 degrees of dihedral as per the plan, we were looking good. The dihedral is the upward angle from horizontal of the wings or the tailplane, looking longitudinally along the aircraft.

With tailplane fitted we were getting ready to go, but the weather was on the turn. Rain lashed against the workshop door and it was evident we were not going to be flying that night. We put the whole structure on the scales for a check; everything seemed good, and loaded with lead, we were at a flying weight of about 137kg with a 30% aft centre of gravity, giving the new Colditz Cock just the correct balance.

Chapter 5

Colditz Here We Come

When the courier failed to arrive I realised that I was starting to feel the pressure and becoming not a little exasperated. We had worked so hard to have everything prepared for this moment and now we had to wait on others.

We were down to the final hours. The weather was not conducive to test flying prototypes and there I was waiting for a courier. I felt very downcast. Was it really going to come down to this; were we doomed to not fly our prototype? It was a fact that the LBA would not allow us to fly the glider from the castle before we had conducted a satisfactory test flight.

I phoned the courier, only to learn that he hadn't even left London. There was nothing I could do. The situation was beyond my control so I thought I would make the most of the enforced delay and set off with my parents to enjoy a Mother's Day celebration. However, on getting out of the car my phone rang – the courier would be at the workshop within thirty minutes!

I begrudgingly returned to the workshop to open up, stomach rumbling. I waited, and waited. Thirty minutes had passed, an hour came – enough of this – I phoned the driver. Stuck on the M25 apparently. That was the final straw, I wasn't waiting any longer. I opened the door, stacked all the equipment outside, closed the door, locked up and phoned the Production Manager. By this time it was almost 21.30 hours, and I felt that I had done my duty long enough. The workshop was in a quiet neighbourhood in a remote location, so it was highly unlikely that anything would be stolen. I also informed the courier that I was leaving the equipment outside the workshop unguarded, which was surely an added incentive for the driver to get there as quickly as he could.

The driver collected the equipment safe and well about 23.00 hours. It was still drizzling, but I had to remain positive. The morning dawned and it was still wet. Nevertheless, I prepared the email for the LBA, just missing the vital flight information. At least the paperwork was all in order for our travels, and with the film equipment now being air freighted to Leipzig, we were pretty set.

It was now just a case of waiting and praying for the weather to improve.

Pat was there, with his transmitter all checked, controls all working. It was balanced, we just needed the skies to clear. To pass the time we had some dregs of dope left and, with the weather not improving and the fact that we had the weight allowance, all hands set to the brushes to dope the top surface of the wings, tail and fuselage sides. We were finishing off as the sun was beginning to set. A check out of the door confirmed the drizzle was slowing – was this our chance? The forecast for Saturday showed yet more rain, this could be it – let's try.

We opened the big workshop doors and four of us picked up the machine. Being based on a small private grass airstrip, we had the place to ourselves. A colleague with a big 4x4 offered to tow.

Whilst the rain had turned to a light drizzle, there was a very low cloud, almost down to tree-top height. This meant that all we were going to be able to manage was ground skids. By law we couldn't fly the machine freely to any height without first informing the CAA and it was too late to do that now, so a slide was all we could conduct. We wanted to record the lift-off speed, so with mirrors trained on the

---

Opposite top: Viewed from the Upper Terrace of Colditz Castle, the landing ground of our flight can be seen on the opposite side of the River Mulde. The PoWs at Colditz had intended to use the same area for their escape flight, though there was far less development and housing in this part of the village during the war. (Dr Hugh Hunt)

Opposite bottom: The landing site as seen from the clock tower at Colditz Castle. Note how uneven the roof line of this part of the castle is – as well as the proximity of the chimney on the left. (Author)

machine we quickly tied an aero-tow rope to the back of the 4x4, took out the slack and we were ready.

Pat confirmed he was all set, and thankful for the damp grass giving some lubrication to the take-off run, I was ready to see if it would work. A small group had assembled for this moment – a moment that would determine our likelihood of ultimate success. If it worked I would immediately complete our paperwork submission for the LBA, and it would mean that I could actually give Hugh some solid data to work from. I had, from previous experience, asked for his initial calculations to be based on a lift-off speed of forty knots. This was a fairly reasonable speed for a machine of this size and weight to lift off and have a suitable safety margin to account for the increasing profile drag the large airframe would suffer from as it becomes detached from the source of propulsion – this test would see if I was right.

The all clear was given, and with much shaking the glider slid forward. The ground run was long, longer than I anticipated, but suddenly it gracefully lifted in a very flat attitude to an altitude of about ten feet. It was stable, but as it accelerated I could see Pat being compelled to continuingly apply left aileron and rudder. Was it a wing twist, or was it the light 90-degree crosswind?

With the rope slack, the rings dropped away and Pat brought the glider down gently. The nose bowl detached on contact with the long grass on the side of the strip and deceleration was rapid. The rest of it though was in one piece. The lift-off speed, at thirty-eight miles per hour, or approximately thirty-three knots, was under my estimate – though it was a good enough safety factor for me. The schoolboy in me said try it again to get another lift-off speed, in true homage to speed records. With the glider and our small group of excited followers at the western end of the airstrip, this was my opportunity to try in the other direction.

With the light fading fast, we quickly turned the glider around and reattached the rope. We didn't bother with refitting the nose bowl, we simply lined her up for another go. Gunning the 4x4, the glider launched quickly. Again it lifted off flat, but this time Pat took it to around twenty feet. He appeared to have considerably greater control but the drift from the south was winning over Pat's attempt to keep it on its easterly heading. As the speed was increasing, we could see the elevator trailing edge fluttering and despite Pat's efforts to keep full up elevator in, the airflow was too great and was reducing the elevator to neutral.

Inevitably, when the power came off the 4x4, and the rope detached, the lack of elevator authority meant that our glider arrived with a slight nose down attitude. The strengthened keel beam dug in and broke away from frames 1 to 5, taking the bottom strut mounts with it. As the glider slid along the airstrip, the struts, now free from the keel, dug in and detached completely, allowing the wing tips to collapse to the ground. From my vantage at the other end of the airfield it looked ominous, but actually, when we unbolted the wings and laid it out the damage wasn't too bad at all – if we could get away with that in Germany, I would be happy. It meant that the incredible idea of escaping from Colditz by aircraft just might have worked.

The test had been highly successful. Again the glider lifted at around thirty-three knots, so we knew a good minimum target for Hugh. We also knew the elevator control needed better authority and, potentially, some further stiffening. We also realised that with the big ailerons, and small rudder, controllability was an issue and we really did need maximum control range as per the plans.

With the remains recovered to the workshop, a quick look over showed that the repairs we needed to perform were minimal. So slight indeed was the damage, we could get the glider up and going again if needed. I hoped we didn't, but a plan formed in my mind. If the absolute worse happened in Germany, and we dropped our attic built version from the roof, this could be an emergency replacement. For a fleeting moment I considered loading it in the trailer and taking it with us, but common sense said otherwise. For the moment at least, the data was sent to Germany, to the LBA and our inspector out there, and the workshop tidied up.

With less than forty-eight hours to departure time, we had done it – we knew it would fly. Racking my brains for simple solutions to the problems we had found, I decided that on the castle machine we would move the control arms of the elevator further outboard. The attachment for the nose bowl needed to be more substantial and, if anything, we needed to restrain 'Alex', the 'pilot', as he had chinned himself on the cockpit forward coaming in the landing.

Pat dropped off some kit for us to take by road; he was scheduled to fly out with some of the production staff on the Monday. Hugh, the Director, and the Editor were flying out on Sunday. Ben, Jess and myself were going to drive, leaving Sunday afternoon and driving overnight to

Opposite: A small scale test being carried to determine the likely acceleration of the glider once launched using the bath tub method. (Ben Watkins)

Above: A close-up of the release hook that would be fitted to the nose of the glider seen here during testing. (Author)

Below: Further tests on the release mechanism being carried out by Dr Hugh Hunt on the Upper Terrace at Colditz. (Regina Thiede)

get to Colditz at lunchtime on the Monday. Ben spent Saturday heading north to the British Gliding Association conference in Nottingham, so I was left sorting out customer emails and planning the work schedule for the workshop in my absence. I was conscious of leaving the workshop for two weeks with limited means of communication; this worried me. I knew it would be in capable hands though, so with no more to be done, I too went home to rest and prepare for the next day.

On 4 March we convened at the workshop. Having had a full and leisurely Sunday lunch I was replete and relaxed. Jess had packed, but Ben had been delayed by the previous evening's social activities and had only arrived home around thirty minutes before we needed to leave to catch the Channel Tunnel booking I had made.

With much urging and encouragement, we left within about twenty minutes of the time I had wanted and set off for Dover. All excited, we soon found ourselves in France, in serious gales. At the first petrol station outside Calais, we stopped to fill the main and two reserve tanks I had in the truck. The information screen at the tunnel exit said that gales in the Channel had cancelled the ferries, and I was glad that I had taken the more expensive, but quicker and less weather-affected, tunnel option.

Leaving Calais towards Brussels and on to Holland, it fell to me to undertake the bulk of the night drive. Ben had fallen asleep in the back, and although Jess did her best to keep me awake as I fought the winds between Calais and Dunkirk, she too soon fell asleep, leaving me to drive quietly with my own thoughts as I towed the monster trailer behind me.

As the hours and kilometres passed slowly I regretted offering to take the first shift at the wheel and I felt myself getting increasingly tired. My usual trick of bananas and water wasn't working. As we reached Eindhoven I heard Ben stir – the perfect time to hand over the reins to him. Having swapped places, I crawled into the back and was asleep the very moment he pulled back out onto the motorway.

By daybreak we were in Germany. With the weather much improved and another fuel stop completed, I took over the wheel once again after Paderborn to complete the final leg into Leipzig and down to Colditz. Turning off the motorway after the airport, we were soon crossing the open fields near Grimma and began searching the skyline for the first sight of the castle. In my mind I had pictured that iconic scene of an imposing *Schloss* Colditz sitting on top of a hill; it never occurred to me that we would need to look down into a valley to first see it.

Consequently, the initial sight any of us had of this famous building by gazing down onto its roof as we descended into the valley – although this did nothing to reduce the impact on us that this imposing structure had. Passing the railway station in the town, the route by which the majority of prisoners arrived at the castle, you could well imagine how they would have seen the castle themselves.

We pulled up around the back of the castle and phoned Uli Pflanz, the production team's translator and production coordinator. The crew was already in the process of initial filming with Hugh in the castle courtyard, and, whilst they finished this and broke for lunch, we were dispatched to our hotel in town for showers and lunch ready for our debut that afternoon.

It was suggested early on that we drive the car and trailer combination right up to the entrance to the prisoners' courtyard, but with a total length of fourteen metres of vehicle, and some very small, narrow, historic gates and arches to get through, this was a slow and careful process. Luckily we got it right on the first take, and having done our first pieces to camera, we were introduced to the castle's guides and management before I was taken up for my first view of the attic.

The castle had largely been retiled during the years since the war. Externally the walls were painted and in good condition, but internally it was a very different story. Our attic space at least had been furnished with a new wooden floor and, under strict instructions to keep it looking new, we were going to have to work carefully to ensure that this happened. Keen to get on, but with exhaustion creeping in, we decided to unload the car and trailer of our tools, materials, and equipment and call it quits for the day. Everybody on the production team got to work unloading and carrying the kit up the spiral stairs and soon we were down to the final pieces, the wing spars.

I am sure there are many theories about the design of the glider, and where information came from as to the required sizes of wings to keep the machine aloft, but here I think we can definitively prove why one factor in the wingspan could only be determined by brute force. Luckily, we had taken the decision to trim the spars exactly to size in the UK before departing for Germany. However, having walked up the steep staircase, I already had an idea as to our first stumbling block, in that there was no apparent easy way to get a sixteen-foot length of timber up a small staircase. We were aware that the spars had come over from the theatre on the other side of the courtyard, so we knew that getting them up the stairs had not been a problem for the PoWs.

Construction work begins on the runway for our glider high above the prisoners' courtyard. The chapel clock tower can be seen on the right. (Author)

Hugh and I gave it a go. To our delight we found that with careful positioning, and by bending the timber only very slightly around the centre spiral, a sixteen-foot length would just slide almost vertically up the stairway, though this meant scraping the paint from the wall in a number of places on the way up. At the top of the chapel, the stairway tightens slightly, too tight to get the spars around. So we actually had to stop at this point and take the spars into the dormitory area to realign ourselves to get through the metal attic door and pass the spar vertically up the next staircase to go in through the attic door. No mean feat, but proof that it would have been impossible to build a bigger span machine from single lengths of timber. What a great discovery, and it was only the first day.

Eager to start on the proper day of the build, we lost the first few hours to being fitted with radio microphones and having the attic wired and lit for filming. Most of Colditz Castle is without power, and the only way we could get limited power in the attic was by running extension

Above: Early stages of the construction of our second, film, replica underway in the Lower Attic at Colditz. The starboard wing is complete, whilst the port wing, in the left foreground, is still in progress. (Author)

leads from the chapel below. Hundreds of feet of cable greatly reduced the power available as we would find out later in the week, but as the attic windows were small and few in number, it gave us enough light to work by.

Laying out the wing spars, we all set to work preparing the wing ribs and frames for assembly. Pat was tasked with building up the fuselage frames, whilst Ben was to start making the control surfaces. Jess and I worked on the wing ribs and when a suitable number had been made these were assembled on the starboard wing's forward spar. Setting them vertically allowed enough drying time to prepare the port wings ribs and soon we had set enough to mount the rear spar and turn the starboard wing flat.

Squaring up the root rib (the first or innermost rib) allowed the first cross brace to be glued and tacked with pins and by lunchtime Jess and I had the starboard wing square. I moved on to start fitting ribs to the port wing whilst Jess worked on fitting the intermediate ribs to the D-section (the principal section of the wing) of the starboard wing and fitting the leading and trailing edges.

A good productive day was had and we were largely left alone by the TV production team, save a time-lapse camera fitted in the corner of the workshop watching our activities. By dinner time the starboard wing was complete in its construction, whilst the port wing had all its leading edge ribs fitted. Ben had completed both ailerons and Pat had about half of the fuselage frames assembled – feeling very ahead of ourselves we headed back for an early night.

Day 2 dawned and, leaving Jess to continue with the construction of the port wing, I helped Pat by completing the fuselage frames and setting the fin post on our build table. Having learnt from our work on the prototype, there was no way we were going to take the fuselage off the build table until all the braces were in place, so work on the fuselage was slow. Roughly placing all the frames up to the rear wing mount helped and each frame was set square, glued, tacked and allowed to dry before the next frame was set. Before commencing with the front build, cross braces were added to the rear fuselage and the joint gussets were glued and tacked to prevent movement. Day 2 ended with the port wing largely complete and with Ben beginning work on the tailplane. Cockily we again had an early night, after visiting our tunnel-digging friends in the chapel below.

On Day 3 progress was slow, as finally the film crew caught up with us. Firstly, Alex, our pilot, was liberated by the production team as he was to play the part of the Dutch dummy, used to cover for a number of successful escapes made by the Dutch at *Appell*. Equally a morning meeting took me away to work with Hugh and the carpenters who had arrived from the UK to build the runway and supporting framework for the bath drop. Whereas we believed that the prisoners had intended to drop the bath within the confines of the chapel building, we were to dangle our bath from the end of the building over the upper terrace. However, a survey of the terraces revealed cellars present directly under the building, and worry was expressed by all as to the likely issues of dropping steel and concrete onto these cellar roofs. With plans in place for sandbagging the drop area, and initial requirements for the runway decided, most of the team left for the press day meeting whilst I escaped to the attic workshop to join the others.

Interest from the German media was high, and all morning we had been watching news vans and reporters arrive trying to get pictures and

Above: All of the fuselage frames laid out on the floor of the Lower Attic prior to assembly. (Author)

interviews. Although knowing this aspect was important to both the production team and the castle, I did feel great relief by being locked away in the roof where we could be left to work.

Progress in my absence had been good. Jess had completed both wings, save for the metalwork, and Pat and Ben had got most of the fuselage frames in place. A call from the production team requested our presence at the press launch and frustratingly for the build the rest of the afternoon was spent discussing the project with local TV and radio.

Keen to catch up, Day 4 dawned wet and damp. For us the task of bending the fuselage frames into place was on the cards. Carrying out a morning raid on the production office, we liberated its kettle and, having filled up several buckets with water in the kitchen, we made our way back to the attic with our spoils. Plugging the kettle in highlighted the failings in the electricity provision as it instantly tripped out all the rest of the power in the attic. Resetting, we turned off all the lights and began to boil up the water. Pat and I then carried out a careful balancing act of pouring the boiling water from the kettle onto the fuselage longerons and catching all the water before it hit the floor in a redundant bucket. The process was repeated over and over until the wood began to gently sag, and, thanks to Pat's superior knot skills, we slowly began to pull the longerons in.

This process took nearly all day, slowly pulling and pulling, before jigging the frames one at a time relative to the rear fuselage, re-soaking and then setting and tacking. Ben and Jess had thankfully continued with the tailplane and elevator and after a late evening of work we ended by surveying our progress with some satisfaction. At least another day remained in making the tail-surfaces. The fuselage frames were all fitted, but all the forward fuselage work was still needed and we had just seven days left to our first possible launch. Thankfully the metal wing fittings

---

Opposite top: With both wings virtually complete, the fuselage, on the right, is progressing well, as is the elevator next to it. This is the same room that the original Colditz Cock was photographed in at the end of the war prior to its destruction. (Author)

Opposite bottom: The basic structure of the fuselage has been completed and is about to lifted off the build table for the ply covering and skinning to begin. (Author)

were in place, so the first stage of covering could begin in earnest.

Hugh and already expressed some concerns about the hook design and its ability to detach successfully from the glider. He called for some tests, which would equally allow us to determine the level of friction we would experience during launch, and therefore to roughly guess our ability to launch the machine. For this Mike and Dermott knocked up a small section of runway on the upper terrace and I was called upon to build a test rig. This presented me with somewhat of a problem, as the only way to effectively test the friction placed upon the runway by the bottom of the glider would be to build the bottom of the glider. Had we been in the UK then we could have done this without difficulty but we had brought just the materials to build our flying machine, not test rigs. So, in true Colditz fashion, we had to start scavenging.

With such a long and varied past, remnants from the castle's history were to be found littered around in stairwells, corridors and rooms. Crawling up into the attic spaces high above the former British quarters, I came across an area of roof that had previously been replaced and retiled. There, lying in a corner, was an old rotten piece of roof beam. A quick measure and it appeared that it was just slightly greater than the size we needed. Carrying the lump back through the spaces through which I had just clambered, mostly in the dark, was both messy and strenuous, but I returned to the attic workshop triumphant. Furthermore, I had a plan.

With some careful cutting I shaped the bottom of the beam to roughly follow our skid contour. Then by measuring the distance between the rear of the skid and the hook mounts, I could make something that very roughly equated to the dimensions of the keel beam in our own glider. With a solution found, I quickly wrapped it in some excess gingham fabric as we had to disguise the fact that it was merely just a large lump of rotten castle. Having then mounted the hook and landing skid I heaved 'the log', as we had christened it, onto my shoulder and took it down to Hugh on the upper terrace. With strict instructions to return us the skid and hook by early the following week at the latest so we could incorporate those bits into the actual build – I retreated to the attic to continue our main work.

Day 5, Saturday, was going to be an early finish. By now all the crew were on site so the production team was taking us out for dinner in the local public house, and an early start was required to keep us ahead. Jess began straight away on the covering, painting coat upon coat of

Above: The completed elevator and tailplane assembly. (Author)

fabric adhesive across the ribs, whilst Pat and I concentrated on the keel beam and fuselage metalwork. Ben took to tackling the complicated rudder structure now that the remaining controls were complete and with thoughts of a night off, we pushed on happily through the day.

Such was the sociable nature of the teams brought together, that the evening was spent talking of all manner of things and before long it was the early hours of the morning – by which point the publican was keen for us to go home to our beds. Needless to say, the productivity of Sunday morning was not great.

Mixing sore heads and cellulose-based glue fumes in an attic was not a pleasant experience, particularly when we were joined by the production team to film the righting of the fuselage from the build bench. Pat had made an excellent effort with the ply skinning and we felt we had sufficient strength built in to take it off the table, and give us some more bench space.

Jess, the starboard wing covering completed, moved on to covering the port wing. This meant that with our fuselage now the correct way up, a trial fitting of the tail and Ben's completed rudder could be made. Pat tackled the aileron covering whilst Ben and I accurately measured out the fuselage metal work to take the spar fittings and we fixed the cable for the rear fuselage spine. Alignment checks completed, the fuselage was looking pretty square. The tail weight at this time was slightly heavier than the prototype as we had taken the step of adding further strengthening to the elevator to reduce the twisting we had found on the prototype's test flight. Knowing we had a little bit of weight in hand, I put Pat on adding more structural strength to the keel beam in the forward cockpit. The producers had requested that Hugh be able to sit in the glider for some photographs, so a seat needed to be fashioned for this purpose. Distracted by setting up the tail controls, I missed the noise of footsteps on the stairs which signified the arrival of the bags of millet seed and the start of the part of this process I had been dreading.

The whole principle of the millet worried me, more so now that we knew we were very tight on weight. Whereas cellulose dope would evaporate whilst drying, we knew most of the millet would stick to the surface. Worse still, from the interviews given by the former PoWs we knew that the millet re-absorbed water from the atmosphere, which would make it heavier again – what if it rains on launch day?

The heating pot, liberated from the Youth Hostel kitchen[1], was set up in the attic, along with water, millet seed, and a big spoon – all the tools we needed to make our dope. Boiling it up seemed to take an age, as it required a long time for the starch to break down. Turning the heat to simmer, we departed to the canteen for dinner, returning in the evening to continue the process. Leaving Pat and Jess to continue to cover the airframe, it fell to Ben and myself to work out a formulae and establish the correct consistency of the starch to make it work. With Ben delegated to do some pieces to camera, I quickly made up three equal size frames, covered them in fabric and weighed them individually. These were to be my test pieces – hopefully the pieces that, when weighed out after doping, would prove that we wouldn't be able to use the millet, allowing me to use the dope that I preferred.

I coated the first in a single layer of cellulose dope, the second in three layers of cellulose dope, and left them to dry. With Ben having collected a considerable amount of starch from the first batch of millet, we pasted this to the third frame and left it to dry in front of the heater. By now it was pushing the early hours of the morning of Day 7; we were all tired and I was convinced we were going to have to wait until the morning to see the results.

Demonstrating the two doped panels to the crew, we showed that they had indeed sealed the fabric. Though the dope hadn't done much to tighten it, it was at least sealed. I put this down to the ambient temperature of the workshop. Clearing up, I just picked up the millet frame to see how it was drying, and was surprised to find it was indeed dry already. I tapped it, and it was like a drum.

Needless to say I was completely taken aback that it had worked. A silence fell across the workshop, production team and all. Testing it again, I was still in disbelief as it really had worked. It was tight, it had sealed the fabric – but what about the weight? Grabbing the scales, the cameras were set up again, all thoughts of bed forgotten. Weighing out first the cellulose dope frames, then the millet frames showed that millet gave us a weight increase three times that of the doped panels. I quickly did some sums based on the prototype's weight. If we were careful, we could just do it. Balancing the aircraft was going to be tricky, but we had provision within the spare weight to cover the surfaces in millet.

The production company was pleased. Ben was happy that we had achieved historical accuracy. I, on the other hand, was in a state of panic. All our sums had been calculated based on using dope, and flying near the weight we had flown the prototype. Hugh was calculating our required launch speed based on a lighter aircraft. We were going to need more weight and more speed. How was I going to sleep tonight?

Chapter 6

Ready to Roll

Day 7 dawned and I knew we were going to have to make it work. We passed the formulae for the water/millet ratios and boiling time to the kitchen staff, who promised to make the quantities we needed, and set about covering the remaining control surfaces. We were now halfway through our time at Colditz, but the days available to complete the build were rapidly dwindling. Our last day would be lost to clearing the site, and we had set aside three flying days to allow for adverse weather. The first of those flying days was Friday, and here we were on Monday still covering the outer surfaces. It was a case of all hands on deck now, anybody, production team included, that walked into the attic was handed a brush – we just had to get it covered.

It was on Day 7 that I finally met our German inspector, Reinhard Schott, who had advised us during our negotiations with the LBA. He entered the attic with Uli, the production team translator, and seemed very impressed with what we had achieved. Through Uli we communicated that all was according to our previously discussed plan and that if he was happy with the build quality, we had no concerns with our plans. He seemed very pleased and excited with seeing the machine in the flesh as it were, but almost gave the game away when he exclaimed to Uli that it was just like the other one! Hastily brushing that statement aside we discussed a few of the finer points of the control system before he happily signed off on the Permit to Fly – our last legal hurdle had been cleared. Thanking him profusely, upon his departure I headed off to find Ian and proudly announced our legal permission to fly had been issued. The relief on his face was more than evident.

Returning to the attic, I received a call to join the carpenters on the roof to talk through anything specific I needed. Leaving Ben with the millet starch from the previous night and a recently covered aileron, I headed across to the former French quarters to gain access to the roof from there. Harnessed up, I joined them on the roof platform for the first time.

The remarkable scale of the work they had done was incredible. Standing there looking out, it was the first time I appreciated the enormity of what they had achieved, but something worried me. Although we had yet to put this glider together, my memories of the prototype were that it occupied a reasonable size. Standing on the runway, surveying what we had, the proximity of the clock tower was not something I had appreciated. I handed our rope access specialist, Waldo Etherington, a tape measure and persuaded him to abseil from the platform to the clock tower. We then managed to measure out the distance from the clock tower to the centre line of the runway. This measurement came in at around thirteen feet. The glider wasn't going to fit on the runway!

Further abseiling took place, and soon we established that to move the glider clear of the clock tower was going to reduce our take-off run by some six feet – and we only had sixty feet to play with in the first place. Not only was our glider going to be heavier than tested, its take-off run was going to be significantly shorter. I went to break the news to Hugh.

Returning to the attic, I was confronted with another problem – it had become apparent that up there in the highest parts of the castle it was just too damp to use the millet. As the prisoners had anticipated, the millet continued to absorb moisture from the air once applied to the fabric. Whereas our conventional dopes would evaporate during the drying process, the millet seemed to merely set – and with the rain and drizzle falling on the tiles just feet above our heads, as quickly as we moved the millet covered surfaces away from the heater, the fabric would sag again from the high humidity in the attic. We had one last chance. We knew the millet sealed and shrunk the cotton, but how to seal the millet? We tried an aileron again, applying millet in front of the heater, drying it, but then carefully applying a layer of dope to seal the millet from the atmosphere. Taking it away from the heater we all watched and it soon became apparent that this two-part process was working. With a single heater it was going to be slow. It was time to put things bluntly to the production team – more heaters or miss flying.

All our dinners were held in the canteen of the Youth Hostel, formerly part of the barracks used by the German garrison, and this gave the members of all the different working parties the opportunity to come together each night to discuss any issues that had arisen. Dinner that night was tense. With a lack of heaters available to hire, we needed a solution there and then. Ideas were pushed around and it was decided that to give us the best working space possible, we would tent off a small section of the attic with thick theatrical drapes. Placing our one heater in here should give us a warmer and drier climate to continue our build and give us a fighting chance to finish on time.

With an attic full of people, the carpenters quickly set up a basic framework for us to hang the material. In what seemed like a matter of minutes we had a small tented workshop set up with lights and the heater. The space was just big enough to house a wing and the fuselage, and we stowed the port wing that Jess was still covering and set about sealing our fabric. Into the early hours of Tuesday we continued and it now seemed that we had a method that would work. Time, then, for some sleep.

The countdown to our flying day was close and thoughts were turning to the weather. Walking down the streets of Colditz to our hotel, the increasing press presence in the town was noted, manifesting itself in rows of parked cars and media vans.

Our first scheduled attempt to fly was Friday, with Saturday and Sunday as weather backups. Surveying our situation, it was looking tight. First thing on Tuesday it was decided to dispatch Pat to the flying field armed with the transmitter.

We undertook a communication check in the attic reusing the servo packs previously tested on our UK prototype, and everything seemed to work fine. With our landing field some distance from the castle, it was now the time to test for distance. With Uli and Pat positioned with the transmitter in various parts of the field, I held a servo pack out of the window of the upper attic, and thankfully the servos worked

---

Opposite top: The fuselage now has the nose bowl and tailplane fitted. Pat Willis can be seen making adjustments to the fin post. (Ben Watkins)

Opposite bottom: The starboard wing covered and pictured prior to the problems we encountered with the millet coat. (Ben Watkins)

Above: Reinhard Schott, who assisted us through the Luftfahrt-Bundesamt's approval process and ultimately issued our Colditz glider's Permit to Fly in Germany. (Reinhard Schott)

accordingly. We had the range, so now it was time to start to fit out our completed sections.

The millet was proving difficult. With the youth hostel kitchen having delivered several vats of millet to us, the process started by smearing copious amounts of our boiled millet paste across the fabric surfaces. When totally sodden the excess seeds and husk residue were removed from the wing using contoured wooden scrapers. With the heater on full power, this process was repeated on all the exposed surfaces until taught and airtight, whereupon a liberal application of dope was applied to seal the structure. The hours ticked by. First we completed the starboard wing, followed by the port wing and rudder. Then on the Wednesday morning, with the fuselage in, we began on the tailplane and slowly but surely we completed each section.

With all of us suffering from extreme tiredness, we completed the last sections that evening and dismantled our tent. I was really concerned about the weight of our machine, and after discussion with Hugh, we decided that a full weight test ought to be conducted on the launch roof to see what speed we could actually achieve.

Thursday dawned damp, but with prospects of it being fine later. The forecast for Friday, though, was overcast but looked better for Saturday. Sunday was due to be dire, so we had our target dates – Friday and Saturday it would have to be.

Having agreed that a full weight test was called for, during a further meeting with Hugh it had been decided that in order to get the speed off the end of the ramp, we would launch a suitable vessel from the runway filled with water and get our launch speed from that. The only suitable vessel that could be obtained that would take 150 litres of water was a garden recycling bin acquired from a local hardware store. Fitted to a set of skis, the bin was carried to the runway roof and with much plumbing of hoses and acquiring of more garden fittings, a hose pipe was hauled to the roof and, with all taps on maximum, water could slowly dribble into the bin.

By now the town was full of press and media. Reporters from various British newspapers had started arriving from the UK, keen to interview members of the team. Whilst we didn't want the distraction, we were contractually obliged to participate, so it was decided we would take it in turns to meet all the journalists at the same time so that work could continue in the attic.

We undertook a late morning visit to the runway to view the completed structure and, I have to confess, it was a magnificent sight. Standing on the end looking over the town, I could see the once sleepy community of Colditz was crawling with people. It would be obvious to them as well as us that the weather favoured either Friday or Saturday, and if we didn't emerge tomorrow, the place would really fill up on Saturday. Turning our attention back to the runway, the surface was rough – much rougher than would be ideal.

We had previously removed the metal skid we had fitted to the glider, and we had already begun to strip out anything we didn't consider essential. Nevertheless, I was still concerned that the friction present in our earlier test would be exaggerated without the skid, but a solution was at hand.

The castle was full of tin guttering and I was convinced that the prisoners would have plated the bottom of their main skid with this tin,

hence why we had carried a metal skid with us for ours. We could, however, get the same effect by covering the runway surface with sheet aluminium, whilst leaving our glider skid as bare wood. This idea met with approval by those around us, and indeed it was suggested in true prisoner manner that blocks of lard 'liberated' from the youth hostel kitchens could be used to grease the runway before take-off to give us a bit of extra friction reduction.

Hugh was correspondingly dispatched to the hardware store and I returned to the attic. On my way I passed Tom and Ian who said they were about to come and film us rigging the glider. Startled by this, I ran up the stairs to the loft. Although we had the main sections complete, we hadn't begun any setting up of the machine. Indeed we had yet to drill out the dowel sections for the tailplane and set its incidence – although it looked complete, it was far from it. Quickly tidying up, we heard the footsteps of the film crew approaching. We resigned ourselves to getting this bit of filming out of the way as quickly as possible so that we could then rig, weigh and ballast the machine whilst setting up the controls – at which point we would be a stage closer to flying.

Positioning ourselves as per the photograph of the original glider in the very same attic sixty-seven years previously,[1] we cautiously brought all the pieces together. Realising that we actually hadn't trialled any of these parts yet, there was considerable relief when the wings bolted together nicely. Easy in a large attic space, but Ben and I in particular, familiar with rigging standard gliders, realised the job we faced rigging the glider on a two-metre-wide platform on the castle roof.

With both wings fitted, the size of the machine we had created became apparent to all. The attic also filled up as more of the castle's staff came to visit, and whilst Ben and Jess fitted the tailplane and rudder loosely we all stood back to admire what we had created. I'm not sure whether it is my memory slowly fading, or whether we didn't actually talk that much, but the minutes after hanging the last part on the machine I recall being extremely quiet ones, with little talking. I think we were all pretty much in awe of what sat before us, and more so when compared to the original photograph taken in that same place all those years before with the machine built by the prisoners under

---

Opposite: The end of the runway being worked on high up on the roof of Colditz Castle. (Ben Watkins)

115

Above: The runway construction team take a moment to confer with Dr Hugh Hunt. The gap in the runway, nearest the bottom right of the picture, was the access hatch up on to the structure. (Ian Duncan)

Below: The runway provided the ideal spot from which to take in the scenery surrounding the castle. The author is standing on the left. (Ben Watkins)

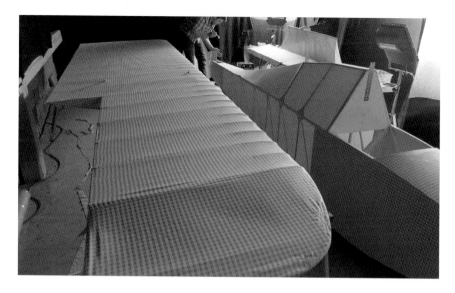

Above: The various sections of the glider inside the tent structure in the Lower Attic. The tent was introduced to allow the team to heat a small area of the room to a temperature high enough to enable the millet coating on the fabric to dry properly. (Ben Watkins)

Below: With the deadline fast approaching for the final flight, the runway construction team was forced to complete its work at night. (Ian Duncan)

vastly different, and more trying, conditions. Many photographs were taken, including the inevitable team picture, followed by a few minutes to camera about the next steps we had to do. Then, as fast as everyone had turned up, they were gone.

Joe returned a short time later with the three mini cams the crew wanted to rig on the airframe. These were duly attached to various parts of the glider. Casually, I said it was about time we crunched the numbers to see where we were with the weight. So, armed with two sets of scales, a spirit level, measuring tape and a pen and paper I set about the task.

Heaving the forward fuselage on to the front scale was no problem, but when Ben lifted the tail to a position that had the fuselage level, he expressed concern at the weight on the rear structure. We took our readings – our model, without ballast, was 20kg heavier on just the empty weight alone. Measuring out the distances between the reaction points, I stuck all the numbers down on a sum to try to see where we came with ballast. We had set ourselves thirty per cent of mean chord as the ideal balance point for the model. I crunched the numbers once more and came out at a figure about 110 per cent of maximum permitted. I tried it again, this time working it out in reverse – though the result still came out with about a forty per cent error on our ballast. I looked at Ben, handed him my workings and set about it all yet again. For certain, to get the ballast we wanted, we were going to be grossly over-weight to the tune of 17kg, and with an all up weight just over 30kg more than our prototype.

By this time Joe had stopped what he was doing – he knew something was wrong. We quickly explained that as the machine stood we couldn't legally fly it. He asked what we were going to do about it. I said that I would do my best to solve the problem, but at the end of the day, we had a set limit and I couldn't be sure I could get it under that. Apologising that he simply had to get this on camera, he rushed off to get the film crew and left us to it. I looked at the guys – it was time to strip all the weight we could. Anything that could come off, had to come off.

Leaving Ben, Jess and Pat to start weighing individual components, I sat there with yet more sums. As part of our insurance and permit application, I had made a damage report analysis for certain crash situations, including impact with roof structures in the town. Our fibre glass nose was light and only affixed with some self-tapping screws,

Above: The two individuals who can be seen standing in the proposed landing field on the opposite side of the River Mulde are in fact undertaking a transmission test to ensure that the glider's remote control equipment would operate satisfactorily at these ranges. (Author)

and I had chosen by design to incorporate the ballast blocks on the rear of Frame 1, keeping them inside the fuselage and hopefully containing the heavy items safely in an impact rather than projecting them forward out of the plane, scattering them haphazardly. Eyeing up the machine, I realised we could actually move our ballast point forward right into the very nose of the machine, further than I had really planned to, but thinking I could substitute lead weights here for water, any penetration of the nose in an accident would lead to the dispersing of the water ballast releasing most of the energy compared to that contained within a lead brick. Moving the weight forward would reduce the amount of ballast needed, which would help. Hearing mutterings in the background, the guys had ripped out around 1.5kg of structure, but this still wasn't going to be enough. Jess weighed the spare controls we had

Opposite top: Virtually complete, our second, filming, replica is pictured in the Lower Attic at Colditz. It is in fact sitting on a pair of scales to weigh it to ensure that the centre of gravity was correct and that the maximum weight set by the Luftfahrt-Bundesamt had not been exceeded. The nose bowl has been left off to allow final adjustments to be made. (Author)

Opposite bottom: The film crew fit cameras to the glider in preparation for recording its big flight. (Ben Watkins)

---

brought over from the prototype, but the difference was not really measurable on the digital scales we had. The millet it seemed was our downfall – it was just too heavy.

The TV crew arrived to film the proceedings. I knew I needed more time, I was determined I wasn't going to let this defeat me, we had come too far. Talking with the Director we called off any chance of flying for the next day. The weather we knew was likely to be better for Saturday anyway, and on top of our serious weight issue, we had still yet to do the full scale water test. Furthermore, the rope access guys had yet to complete the rig of the loft and launch runway for getting our machine out. Too many problems were lining up, we needed to sacrifice a launch day.

I started moving the balance point back; with every few percent the ballast required got lighter and lighter. Ideally you want the machine to balance at or just forward of the centre of pressure produced when the wing creates lift. The further you get behind this, the more unstable and relatively un-flyable the machine becomes. Weighing up all the lead blocks we had, together with accounting for about fifteen litres of water being roughly the maximum I could get in the front, I knew what my ballast limit was, and with each movement of the centre of gravity aft, we got closer and closer to our magic 150kg maximum. With a balance point of forty-seven per cent of mean chord, and maximum ballast, the calculator said we could do it and weigh in at 149.3kg. I didn't know if it was even possible for a conventional design high wing aircraft to fly with a centre of gravity that far aft and a quick look on the internet did not reveal any supporting evidence. We wanted to be legal, but we wanted it to fly as well.

I pulled Pat aside. He was cautious as he had the same concerns as I about control effectivity. Flying in the condition now proposed, the nose would be a lot higher than we would want for normal gliding flight. The wing incidence had already been set and we were worried that in its new balanced state, we would be close to the stall position. Luckily, in our rush to rig for the cameras we had yet to set the tailplane incidence, and this we could use to our advantage. By reducing the angle of incidence of the tail, we stood a chance of getting some controllability back. Instead of the usual two degrees of negative incidence the drawings called for, we settled at zero degrees incidence, and wound the elevator throws up to maximum in both directions. By now I needed suitable containers to carry water as ballast, but the store was shortly to close. That problem would have to wait for the morrow.

News then came from our colleagues on the roof that the full weight bin test was not far from happening, so we decided to see what fate would await the latest test rig. Meeting the castle caretaker on the way to the terrace, he insisted that a much better view could be had from a small parapet high on the roof of what had been the French quarters.

With the caretaker as our guide, we arrived shortly before a pleasant sunset. Listening in to the radio chatter, it seemed Waldo was greasing up the newly-installed sheet metal runway, but the water bin was full and was about to be attached to the bathtub. After what seemed like an age, the bathtub was lifted to a considerable height, the rope was attached to the bin and the release trigger was set. Waldo and James released the safety rope from the bathtub, and everything was armed. The sun had set and the evening was quiet and peaceful. It was only the occasional radio chatter whilst cameras were focussed, or the shuffling of feet as people were moved safely out of the way, that broke the silence. In the town below a family was having a barbeque, the smell of which was drifting up to the castle – I wondered if they knew of our antics far up above their heads.

Hugh, of course, was very aware of what we were doing, and as our intention was to simply confirm the speed we could get with 150kg propelled by bathtub, he tethered the bin to ensure it stayed within the castle grounds. Just as the light faded we heard the 'all clear' be called

---

Opposite: Looking down from the former French PoW quarters, this image gives an impression of the drop involved in the bath tub method of launching and accelerating the glider off the rooftop runway. (Ben Watkins)

and shortly after we were greeted with the sight of our bin hurtling off the end of the castle's roof.

All went well until the tether caught tight, at which point the bin up-ended, ejecting the load of water it was carrying with such force that it took out one of the castle's floodlights. The whole event was met with much mirth by the glider team – perhaps it was tiredness from a long day, but we all collapsed in hysterics. Anyway, recovering our decorum, we knew we were close to making the Saturday for flying, though the next day would be critical.

Friday duly dawned. The main tasks facing the team were to tidy the fabric edges and secure the camera mounts for the next day. Uli took me down to the local DIY store to search for water containers. I wanted soft collapsible containers, that would mould to fit the front of our glider, but unfortunately none could be found. I did locate some lighter solid plastic containers which in fifteen-litre volumes would fit nicely in our nose bowl – so that's what we came away with. A quick visit to the landing field (my first visit) showed that the grass was being freshly cut. The castle sat imposingly above us and I could clearly see Mike and Dermot checking over the runway from our bin escapades the night before and preparing the rigging for getting the glider out of the attic and onto the roof.

Returning to the castle, I stopped off in the kitchens to fill the water tanks. When I got to the attic, the team had almost finished all the final fabric trims on the glider. It was still rigged so we were able to add ballast and conduct our final weight and balance and centre of gravity checks, settling with a forty-seven per cent mean chord balancing point – far from ideal, but legal at least.

Opposite top: The author's comparison of the famous wartime photograph of the original Colditz Cock in the Lower Attic – see Chapter 2. The windows that can be seen in the US Army image were blocked up in the years after the war. (Author)

Opposite bottom: The replica Colditz Cock construction team pose for the camera with Dr Hugh Hunt (who is kneeling in the centre whilst holding a copy of the wartime image of the original glider). Standing, from left to right, are Pat Willis, Jess Nyahoe, the author, and Ben Watkins. (Ian Duncan)

The time had come to open the roof. The carpenters, having completed the construction of the runway, had moved into our attic space. They were then busy taking off the roof tiles and cutting the roof battens between two roof beams in the far corner. Jim and Waldo had rigged a couple of ropes that linked the clock tower and British quarters with the glider attic and theatre building. Although originally the prisoners had planned to take the wall out above the launch roof, we weren't allowed to damage the historic brickwork. The rope access team planned to haul the wing out on one line, connect it to a second line to lift it up to the clock tower, pass it through the gap onto a third line and out then onto the rooftop runway – it made sense, but at the time I still couldn't picture what they wanted to do.

As for the glider itself, we had finally reached the culmination of our build. We now had to de-rig the glider carefully in the attic and we stacked it around the room in the order we wanted to get it out. We then strapped in our 'pilot' – at which point we realised that there was little else for us to do. Virtually none of our parts could fit through the personnel access in the runway, except for the water ballast, lead weights, and nose bowl – these we transported through to the loft under the runway. 'Alex' was strapped into the seat and we tied up the lift struts to the underside of the wing.

With little left to do, the sensible thing was to head off to bed. I found myself fumbling around the loft. We really were on the verge of flying and all eyes were looking to us to deliver on what we had set out to achieve. Even though everything seemed to be in place I could not help but feel anxious. I thought there must be more that needed checking. Were our recommendations correct? Was our plan to rig it going to work? The production team was so trusting of our suggestions, but everything had been going around in my own head so much that I began to doubt myself. Nevertheless, Uli confirmed with the media, town authorities, and fire team that the time had come – we were flying tomorrow.

Chapter 7

To the Skies

We convened outside our hotel at 04.45 hours the next morning. It was still pitch black and with only the light of the moon we made our way up to the castle for 05.00 hours. I hadn't slept much, and although the others looked fresh. I knew they too had their own nerves and probably had been as restless as I. Ben, Pat, Jess and I met quickly outside the production office. I nominated Ben and Pat to man the launch roof, as they were the ones who had to receive the glider parts from the rope specialists Jim and Waldo. Jess and I were to haul the parts out of the loft. This was not a strenuous task, but if it was going to go wrong anywhere, it was going to be here and I wanted to know all about it.

Ten minutes later, the whole crew met to discuss the plan for the coming hours. Everybody had their own jobs, but equally we had cameras to fit, activate, or man – the commissioning TV channel had their own criteria for photographic records, and the newspapers also wanted our attention. Everyone shook hands – we certainly needed all the luck for what was coming up – as this was the last time we were all going to be together until the flight was over.

After the meeting I pulled aside the Executive Producer. I asked him what was his criterion for success? He said: 'When it leaves the roof using a bathtub, we have a programme. If it crashes never mind. If it crashes in the field, that's better. If you guys can land it in the field, that's better than we all imagined – but please whatever you do, try not to damage anything, none of us want an insurance claim now!'

Climbing the stairs to the attic with Jim and Waldo, we discussed our own safety. Working out on the roof ledge in the early morning dew

and lit by the rising sun, we didn't want accidents to happen. Jim rigged a safety line in the roof of the attic and I clipped myself to it. The tail parts we knew were already in the Lower Attic under the launch runway, we simply had to get two wings and a fuselage out – but that was much easier said than done.

The port wing went out first. With a control line tied to the spar, there it was, the fruits of our labour dangling out over the courtyard. Through a method of tightening and slackening several lines, we managed to haul the wing around, clipping it one fastener at a time onto the crossed line and soon we had turned it around through ninety degrees and it was sliding up to the clock tower. An instant later, it was passed over onto a third line to make its way down to the launch runway. From this point on it was out of my view.

A radio call from Ben on the other side confirmed they had received it safe and well, and the sling was coming back to us – no damage, and no problems – or so I thought. What I didn't realise was that although the sun was coming up and was bathing the attic in bright warm sunshine, poor Ben and Pat were deep in shadow and had yet to receive the warming effects of the sunlight. I did find out much later though that they did receive the warming effects of a pot of tea, and whilst Jess and I were struggling to get the fuselage out of the loft, they were merrily slurping back a cuppa.

The only strong points we had on the fuselage were the wing mounts and the fin post, so that's how we had to sling it. Unfortunately being much longer than a single wing panel, the fuselage had to hang much further out over the courtyard, and by the time we had man-handled it out onto the cross cable, we were getting pretty tired.

My heart nearly stopped as it headed between the clock tower and the roof apex – the wings although long, were thin, but with the fuselage we ran the risk of scraping the delicate side fabric on the brickwork as it passed by. Waldo's solution was to lift it high – almost out of everyone's reach.

Thankfully after some clever negotiation it was on the runway, and Ben was instructed to begin installing the water ballast in the nose. With the final wing in the sling, our last act in the attic was to repeat the

---

Opposite: The last few steps in the construction of the runway are completed. The author can be seen on the right. (Ben Watkins)

129

Above: Launch day, and the rigging and runway undergoes its final checks. (Ben Watkins)

Opposite: The difficult task of moving the glider parts from the attic out on to the roof begins – in this case the wings. Part of the runway can just be seen to the left of the clock tower. (Regina Thiede)

process of the first wing, something we achieved with greater ease and confidence.

Jess headed off to get her harness for the runway roof, leaving me to survey our now empty attic. After the hectic bustle of previous weeks, the late nights and the bonding that had gone on between all of us, it seemed a very empty place now. My thoughts were interrupted by a radio message which alerted me to the fact that all the pieces of the glider were now on the roof – would I kindly join the others.

Rushing down the spiral stair case, across the yard, and up the staircase of the French quarters, I arrived in the Lower Attic. Keith, the

Opposite: The wing is carefully manoeuvred between the tower and the attic roof, the crew keen to avoid damage to either the structure of the castle or the glider itself. (Regina Thiede)

Above: The glider's fuselage breaks out into daylight for the first time. (Regina Thiede)

---

sound man, had positioned himself just off the loft attic and he greeted me with his usual beaming smile. Climbing the short ladder to the skylight and then hauling myself along underneath the runway structure to make my way out through the hatch onto the runway surface, I was greeted by the team resting amongst the glider parts. By now daylight was upon us and so we had to crack on with rigging.

Both Ben and myself were experienced glider pilots, very familiar with the ins and outs of rigging gliders from trailers, but normally in the comfort of big grass fields. On a two-metre-wide platform, six stories high on a castle perched on a precipitous slope was another matter. Jess had worked for me for the previous year and was getting more familiar with the task, but space on the roof was tight. There were two safety

ropes running the length of the runway, with a maximum of two people clipped to each rope. Pat was clipped to the wall, and Hugh to a set of ropes at the end of the runway. The wings themselves were as wide as the platform we stood on, and with Jess being the smallest of the group, we gave her the task of securing the fuselage. Pat would help support the tip and we accosted Hugh to help where needed.

Spinning the fuselage around so both the nose and tail hung over the drop, we carefully lifted the wings one at a time up to the wing fixings, and then with Ben and myself supporting the fuselage, Jess could crawl

---

Opposite: Seen this time from the runway on the attic roof, the wing is manhandled towards the final assembly point. (Dr Hugh Hunt)

Below: With the first of the glider parts, the wings, having safely reached the giddy heights of the runway on launch day, Hugh Hunt, second from the right, discusses the next step with members of the assembly team. (Dr Hugh Hunt)

Opposite: A slightly more difficult proposition than the wings, the fuselage is also fed through the gap between the attic roof and the tower. This image provides a clear view of the glider's skid. (Regina Thiede)

Above: The fuselage pictured having negotiated the worst part of its journey to the runway. (Dr Hugh Hunt)

Below: Ben and Pat receiving the fuselage on the runway. (Dr Hugh Hunt)

underneath to fit the wing struts at their lower attachments. If that wasn't difficult enough, we then had to turn the glider around to face down the runway. This sounds simple, but with no wing supports we were having to support the whole airframe by the lower struts to stop it falling off the building whilst the carpenters hastily made some wing stands to support each wing outboard of the strut fittings.

Activating the wingtip cameras before swinging them over the drop, Ben and I found ourselves having to sit on the edge of the runway, our feet dangling over the roof edge with the struts resting on our thighs whilst the carpenters got to work.

The wind was getting up, though we had known it would from the forecast. Soon with the sun beating down, the thermals would start and with the runway in shadow and the castle courtyard in full sun, the turbulence caused by the rising air would make our problem worse. Personally, I was now hating the situation. I desperately wanted it to be over and done with. In fact, the longer I sat there, and it seemed like an age, the more I wanted to just tip the whole machine over the edge and just call the day at an end. I looked across at Ben, his face said it all – and later he confirmed he was thinking exactly the same as I. In all the situations I had been in, this was by far the most exciting, uncomfortable, and terrifying all at the same time. Eventually the wing stands were in place and we could relax – although they needed to be a bit higher as the machine was able to bounce between the two.

I thought if we were quick and could get everything ready to go, we could probably get it flying before the wind caused any damage. With the tail fitted, it was time for a quick control check with the transmitter to ensure all was in order, at which point our time on the roof was over. As we made our way around the machine to unhook and make our way down, the first delay of the morning occurred. Official publicity photos of the team had to take place on the roof, and the photographer was still not at the castle. I was not best pleased.

We waited, and waited, and finally the man arrived in the clock tower to photograph us all. My usual pleasant nature had deserted me, and after a minute or two of smiling for the camera, I announced it was time

---

Opposite: The fuselage is prepared for the fitting of the wings. The large wooden post on the right was removed once all the sections were in place, part of the process of preparing the runway for the take-off. (Author)

Above: Work to complete the final assembly continues rapidly. Here the wings have been fitted to the fuselage. (Dr Hugh Hunt)

to go. I was leaving Ben on the roof as the technically-capable man on the scene; I certainly would need him in the hours to come.

Pat and Jess left the roof before me, closely followed by Hugh. I had one last look at our machine, sat there ready for flight. Just an hour before I had wished the thing had fallen to the ground, but now with bright blue sky above us, the smell of a barbeque breakfast being cooked wafting up from the town below, I realised that after months of work, the toil and effort, the criticism, the doubters, the support of friends and family and the unending help from those around me there, that my work on this project was actually completed right there. I had no other function to perform.

For just a moment I could take in the view, the people lining the bridge in the town, the local officials and invited guests that surrounded the landing field. Then there were the inhabitants of Colditz, watching from their gardens and from the town square. There were *thousands* of people there; I hadn't appreciated just how many people had taken an interest in what we were doing. I could see the fire brigade's motor launch patrolling the river. I could see a few British flags flying in the town – a number of German ones too. That was a moment I will never forget.

I made my way down into the Lower Attic and, ditching the safety gear, I headed through the castle to my car. The minibus had already left with most of the film crew so that they could set up in the field. The place was deserted. Packed just minutes before, now there was just Pat, Jess, and myself. I got to my car, with the trailer attached, parked in the lane to the castle where it had been for the previous two weeks. We made our way down the hill into the town with the trailer which, having brought our tools and materials just a few weeks earlier, was now, with luck, about to pick up our glider from the landing field.

The town was packed and it was difficult making our way across the bridge, but through all the people I could just make out our glider on the runway; I was proud again. Arriving at the field, we were ushered through the crowd and parked up by the landowner's house. In 2012, the landing field was effectively a privately-owned garden, which had now been swamped with camera crews and important local dignitaries.

I left the car and saw Hugh standing with the producer in the field. Making my way over I saw Reinhold, our LBA inspector and the man who had issued our permit some ten days before. He held out his hand and I shook it.

'How did the build go?' he asked.

'Long,' I said. 'It is heavy, but legal!'

He leaned in closer. 'You know, if this goes wrong, we are both in trouble!' he said, adding, 'Good luck,' as we shook hands again.

Reaching Hugh, I was keen to get things moving. With the cameras rolling I called up the producer and asked what we were waiting for. Ben reported everything was 'Ok' on the roof, so the winching of the bathtub began. Safety being foremost through the whole project, meant we had several safety devices in the winching system, which slowed the process of actually lifting the tub. Then, after some ten minutes, the bath was hanging from the glider and the release hook was in place at the back of the skid. I was surprisingly relaxed. My work was done. What happened next could not be decided by me – I just wanted it done before the weather went against us.

Being in a crescent-moon-shaped valley, the wind that had been in a rear quarter to our launch run from first thing that morning was now blowing from the side – which really wasn't going to help the glider lift off the runway. From our previous tests we knew that we were going to be slow off the ramp and I had hoped all week that we would have a headwind, but alas now that the time for flight was upon us, we were

to be denied this luxury. Time was marching on and although we had been charging the battery packs all night Pat was very conscious that we had turned these units on two hours earlier. Although on standby, we didn't want to risk losing a battery pack now.

With everything prepared, the cameras rolling, and the press in place, it was time for a control check, with Ben calling back the results of Pat's inputs over the radio. Elevator and rudder checks went well, but with the aileron inputs for roll applied, we failed to get the required one-up-one down result. We tried again, but again we had little movement from the port aileron. The starboard aileron, we soon determined, was working well, but the port was responding intermittently. I consulted with Pat. The control check on the roof had definitely gone to plan; could we have damaged the pack somehow during turning the glider around? It was more likely that with the wings now sitting on wooden supports, and the glider being bashed around by the winds buffeting it from all sides, something had become dislodged on the control panel.

Deep in thought, it was clear that we needed to determine if damage had occurred to the panel. Ben couldn't see anything from his vantage point, but Pat was the man who had designed and put together the control packs, so he needed to be there. Calling on the production team, I dispatched Pat in the van to go back to the castle to see what he could do. In a flash of people, cameras and photographers, I suddenly found myself pretty much on my own in the field, with the vast majority of people now heading to the castle, or already on the roof, even the radio was quiet.

Pat arrived on scene and from a skylight on an adjacent roof, directed Waldo to abseil from the clock tower to examine the troublesome unit. Nothing seemed too apparent from first inspection and, actually, back in the castle the power pack seemed to function perfectly. It was decided that perhaps there was an intermittent fault with the primary servo on that pack, and that the secondary servo could become the prime unit, with the suspected troublesome unit being isolated. This switch worked and, with the controls functioning perfectly, the party left the roof to join me again in the field.

Opposite: Photographed from below, this view of the glider during its final assembly not only provides a good illustration of the effort involved in constructing the runway, but the lack of space available to the team as they worked high up on the castle roof. (Dr Hugh Hunt)

I had been quietly enjoying some snacks liberated from the dignitaries' buffet lunch when the production team's mini-bus arrived back in the field and spilled out the hoard of camera men and, thankfully, Pat who was armed with his transmitter. The long process of hauling the bathtub up again began – and it couldn't come too soon. We were rapidly approaching early afternoon, hours after we had wanted to fly and the wind was gusting. It seemed to take an age, but strangely I felt very calm. After all it was down to Pat now. He had been an integral part of the team from just a few weeks after the project's conception, but now, with the flight looming, it all rested on his shoulders and for once not on mine. We called up Ben – just one last control check, and we were off.

Rudder, OK. Elevators, OK. Ailerons – failed! Our problem had returned, our port aileron system just wasn't working. All eyes turned to Pat. It had worked when he was on the roof just minutes before. What was wrong?

I tried to ignore for a minute the discussions going on around me about camera battery life. It was clear that we were going to have to change more batteries to keep the remote cameras rolling. There was just one solitary camera on me and I didn't want it. I paced around mulling over all of the possible scenarios. It was evident the batteries were fine as the units were functioning, just not reliably. Everything had been charged that morning and we knew when we tested it that we had the range, and perfect line of sight all the way from the field to the glider on the roof.

Joe the camera man asked what I was thinking, and for the first time I spoke out loud about our problem. Our three packs were charged up, we had verified minutes before that the problem port wing pack would function, but now we found ourselves here struggling to get that pack to work. Studying the scene I suddenly had a thought. From where I was I could clearly see the rudder, and the starboard aileron, but I could not see the port wing. Then the wind blew and it just rose over the

Opposite top: Work on attaching the wings is well underway. (Dr Hugh Hunt)

Opposite bottom: The author takes a moment to check the progress of the fitting of the wings. Note the improvised wooden struts used to support the wings in this process. (Ben Watkins)

runway structure and came into view. An idea dawned, our control effectivity seemed to coincide with the rising and lowering of the wing due to the gusty wind – it wasn't the impacting of the wing on its support stand that was causing us problems, it was the sheer fact that it didn't work when it sat on the stand, out of sight of us in the field. I knew we were right on our signal limit, but surely it wasn't that critical – then the penny dropped.

Days earlier we had decided about the weight-saving idea of placing tin on the roof rather than just on the skid of the glider. We were trying to transmit from such a distance that we were blocking out the last of our signals whenever the wind blew our last receiver out of sight. Ignoring Joe who was trying to ask me questions, I called to Pat to move to the edge of the field closest to the castle. This gave him direct views to both sides of the runway and about 100 yards nearer the castle itself. A call to Ben for a control check and that was it, it worked. We had sorted it.

I suddenly felt terribly sick. Although this was now our third attempt to launch, and I'd been fine previously. Something now actually told me that this was it – we were about to go. In a quiet corner of the field, Pat stood ready with his transmitter. Hugh, with the radio, was co-ordinating with everyone. Jess was watching intently. As for me, I was trying very hard to keep my stolen breakfast down. Poor Joe the cameraman had to keep his lens on us for our reaction, his back to the castle so that only our facial expressions would let him know what was occurring.

The countdown started. We could think of nothing holding us up, it was about to go. Zero came, but nothing happened. A call from Mike on the roof said that it was too windy and the release unit wasn't working. Still nothing, the seconds seemed like minutes. Another call from Mike: 'When the wind stops blowing we will go.' I thought my heart had stopped beating. I was supposed to be checking on the monitor for signs of movement, but instead my eyes were fixed to the rooftop.

Then suddenly it moved.

I doubted myself for a moment that the glider actually moved, but there it was appearing over the rooftop. What was in reality a very quick process seemed so desperately slow to me.

Dipping off the end, of the runway the glider then began descending rapidly. However, I could see that Pat was inputting a roll to starboard but nothing seemed to be happening. Then I heard the crack of the impact of the concrete-filled bathtub as it ploughed into the cushioning pile of timber and sandbags we had lined the lower terrace with to stop the bath passing into the cellars below.

The glider was continuing on its rapid trajectory towards the town, and all my thoughts were on it being too slow off the roof, the tailwind component wasn't helping either, but I knew that if we could reach flying speed, it would indeed fly. Slowly it started to react.

I watched the wings begin to roll, but the tail appeared to still be continuing on its original course, something must have happened. I knew making it light was going to cause problems, but I didn't foresee there being a structural issue at all. I was worried about the amount of twist, but suddenly, as the machine seemed to be almost upon the village, it flicked square to the wings and gracefully the glider arced around towards the landing field.

It looked far to close in to be able to fly the full 180 degrees needed to land into wind. It also looked far too high to make a landing in the field from its current position and I watched as it continued to turn away from me, appearing to be aiming for the river. As it exposed its underside, I could see fabric flapping away from the lower surface of the fuselage structure. I wondered what the cause of this was, but such thoughts were quickly dismissed as I saw that the glider was starting to roll to the left to bring it towards the field. This, I thought, was possibly because Pat was going to attempt a landing downwind into the field.

The glider seemed to be flying fine, and was carrying a reasonable amount of speed by now. It had lost most of its height and, having cleared the trees, I could see it was within the field boundary. The VIPs in the host's house must have had a fine topside view as it passed, but from my position in the corner of the field I was losing sight. I saw the top now rolled over about thirty degrees to Port, with a nose-level attitude, before a sharp pitch forward began at a height of about twenty feet. The wing contacted the ground first, and I thought it was likely to cartwheel, but instead the wings seemed to detach together and the whole thing stopped pretty abruptly within the confines of our target.

I suddenly realised I was on my own. Everybody had set off across the field, running towards the glider. I just stood there for a minute. It really was over. The glider appeared broken, but it had landed and we hadn't damaged anything – and that was what was most important. The pressure and worries of the previous months had now passed. We had done it.

Above: Seen from some distance away, in fact from some ruins to the north of the castle, the glider is pictured waiting on the runway prior to the big launch. (Mike Coles)

I enjoyed the fact that I was on my own; I needed just that little bit of time to get my head around what we had just done. We were now a part of the history books, and what had just occurred through the efforts of many people was going to be told. Fabulous. I had a lump in my throat and I could feel a little hint of a tear in my eye, so a slow stroll towards the gathered masses around the glider was much needed.

My solitude was not to last, as suddenly to my left I saw the news reporters running my way, all wanting my immediate reaction so they could get the details back to their respective news desks. Rapidly this was followed by the film crew, also keen to get my feelings about it all. From what I recall it was simply that we had made it to the field, proved the concept worked and that thankfully the project had been a success.

'Alex' probably thought otherwise. The impact of the wing on the ground broke the frame immediately behind him and the mass of

148

Above: One of the cameras set up to catch the glider's flight from as many angles as possible. At the point this picture was taken, the take-off was imminent and the tension and excitement mounting. (Mike Coles)

timber and steel continued forward as the fuselage dug in, snapping his polystyrene head. The show and the papers subsequently made a big thing of the pilot coming to grief during the landing. If I had made him all out of plastic he would have fared somewhat better, as would a human pilot, though much bruised or even injured. I had originally hatched a plan that if he had got out unscathed, we were going to photograph him in his escape gear as he made his way back across Europe and finally to the shores of Britain. This would have made some great ending credits.

The next hour was a blur, with lots of hugging and congratulating. The official photographer wanted a group shot, but I stopped proceedings. Ben, the carpenters Mike and Dermott, and Jim and Waldo the rope access guys were still strapped to the roof, and we weren't having any photos until everyone was there. A van was dispatched and

149

Above: Though the glider is battered and damaged, and Alex had seen better days, it has nevertheless successfully completed the flight down from the castle. (Ben Watkins)

Below: Another view of the battered replica 'Colditz Cock' on the landing field beside the River Mulde. (Dr Hugh Hunt)

Above: A jubilant Hugh Hunt is pictured beside the glider after its landing. The distance it covered during its flight can be clearly gauged. (Dr Hugh Hunt)

Above: Time for one of the last pieces of filming, this time undertaken with the knowledge that the project had been a total success. (Dr Hugh Hunt)

---

soon I saw them walking across the field towards us. I saw Ben and I gave my friend a big hug. Of all the people there, Ben knew more than most the sheer level of legislative and technical issues that had been overcome to get us to where we were right there and then.

The crowds and guests soon dispersed. We then brought the trailer into the field, and whilst Hugh and I were taken to one side for interviews, I could see, 100 yards away, the rest of the group laughing, joking, and slowly de-rigging the glider and putting it in the back of our trailer, the trailer that just twelve days before had brought a big pile of timber to the castle, and was now going to triumphantly take back the remains for eventual display.

With the promise of a hearty meal, some local beer and a night of not working, I drove the combination back through the village and up to the rear of the castle. With the *Schloss* closed to the public, we few tired individuals sat in the prisoners' courtyard with a BBQ and several crates of the finest local dark ale. The castle's cooks had even baked us a special cake to mark our time there and for once it was good to talk with people we had lived with for the past few weeks to actually find out about them and not talk about work. The celebration continued into the early hours, courtesy of the local public house which looked after us willingly.

Our attention turned to clearing up, packing up, and returning home. My thoughts were already switching back to my usual work, and this almost unreal experience would soon be a memory, though one that would never fade.

So what had happened on that historic flight? Hugh did some quick calculations that showed we had come off the roof at about twenty-eight knots, not the forty knots we wanted. I put the tailwind component at about eight knots, so really the bath had actually given us an equivalent of twenty knots of thrust relative to the surrounding air, and from our prototype tests, we needed thirty-three knots just to fly, so that would explain why it took so long to gain flying speed from the ramp. Luckily, with having lots of photographers at different places to record the flight, reviewing the photographs, and the damage incurred to the airframe, was pretty easy. It was soon clear what caused our structural problems, partly my design, and partly because of physics.

The original plans show diagonal braces fitted between the frames between the longerons in both the fuselage sides, and the lower fuselage surface. The top was braced only by electrical cable – or in our case seven-strand steel wire. All good so far, and built as per the plans.

As we were holding the entire bathtub weight on the glider, we had to somehow restrain the latter. This was done by welding a ring onto the back of the skid. This ring fitted into an old Air Ministry bomb release, which was activated by a lever and pin, and had worked very well on our test log, it being designed to work under high load and it was a good choice of a release. However, as our runway was a simple timber deck, it would not be able to hold our release with the glider and bathtub load applied, so our only option to secure it to something immovable was to drill an eyebolt into the wall of the castle at the back of the launch ramp and loop a 8mm thick steel cable through the release and back to the eyebolt. This took the strain fine, and clipped onto the back of the skid immediately below the rear fuselage, obviously with our ballast weights in the nose, the glider sat with its tail in the air, again no problem.

The difficulty came, however, at the moment of release. As the release let go of the skid, Newton's Third Law came into effect and as the glider

Above: The glider seen from the ruins soon after its landing. Such a picture leaves you contemplating what might have happened if the prisoners at Colditz had undertaken the same flight in their own, earlier, 'Colditz Cock'. (Mike Coles)

accelerated forwards, the release, tethered by its cable, recoiled backwards towards the wall. Combined with the acceleration forces, and therefore the thrustline acting upon the hook which was well below the centre of gravity, the glider naturally rotated back to a tail-low position. The two combined so that as the glider continued forward, the recoiling release entered the rear fuselage and took out all the diagonal cross ribs as far back as the tailplane.

If I had placed diagonal cross braces in the top of the fuselage, the twist would have been taken by these. However, by losing the bottom braces the fuselage sides were only really being held apart by the form of the upper parts of the frames and the gusset plates we had fitted to each joint.

This brought it home to us as to actually how close we had come to snapping the rear from the end of the aircraft. As with many things you can plan, calculate, and speculate for ever and a day but sometimes you just need that little bit of luck to see you through.

Our luck had indeed held and our Colditz Cock had flown beyond the castle confines, just as Bill Goldfinch, Jack Best, Tony Rolt and the others had imagined some seventy years ago. Now we know that the most ambitious prisoner of war escape of the Second World War really could really have succeeded. Incredible.

Appendix

The Other Replicas

THE FIRST FLYING REPLICA
Norfolk and Suffolk Aviation Museum, Flixton, Bungay

The Norfolk and Suffolk Aviation Museum has grown considerably since it was formed in 1972 in a single Nissen hut near the former RAF Bungay. Now with several hangars, smaller buildings, and seventy airframes on display, its place in aviation preservation is significant. Two of these preserved machines are of particular interest.

Nestled in one of the hangars is the Colditz Cock replica built for the prequel to our documentary in 2000. This full flying replica was built in joint co-operation between Southdown Aero Services and John Lee, an enthusiastic and imaginative Engineer and fellow member of the Southdown Gliding Club. I had great pleasure in sharing the airfield at Parham with John many times in the short time I knew him. Regretfully, we only shared a few workshop visits and a couple of dinners at his house before he sadly passed away in April 2003.

John was asked by Mike Fripp, of Southdown Aero Services, to tackle the wings of the 2000 replica, as these were very similar to Hutter 17 wings, of which John had built two in previous years. Southdown Aero Services had six weeks in total to build their replica, which reputedly cost the production company £30,000. Just like we found, Mike and his team found lots of information missing from the drawings. To comply with the regulatory constraints placed on their project, the team, at the same time as constructing the replica to match aerodynamically the design of the Colditz Glider, had to be modified to take significant components from other gliders. The rudder pedal

Above: The Flixton replica pictured in a hangar at the Norfolk and Suffolk Aviation Museum. (Author)

assembly and system came from a German K13, the wing fittings came from a Hutter 17, the tailplane fittings from a Slingsby Cadet, control cables from a Nord 2000, and the seat assembly from a Slingsby T21. With these greater legislative restrictions than we had to deal with, many small changes were made away from the original design, including the fitting of a conventionally sprung main skid and a modern winch hook.

The British Gliding Association (BGA) oversaw the construction of the aircraft. Due to the nature of the design and the mix of parts and systems fitted to it, the glider was given a temporary Permit to Fly with a limited number of flights. To keep the project away from the eyes of the media, all flights were to be conducted within the confines of RAF Odiham, with the BGA insisting that legendary pilot Derek Piggott should carry out the first two test flights. Launching to 700 feet, Derek reported that although sluggish in controllability, the glider actually flew well and he was happy for filming to progress. For filming, John

Lee, the builder of the wings took control, and on 2 February 2000, in front of a number of former PoWs, including Bill Goldfinch and Jack Best, the glider soared up the winch launch for four flights. Immediately post the filming, the glider moved to display at the Imperial War Museum, before taking up residence at the Norfolk and Suffolk Aviation Museum. The glider continues to attract the attention of the many who visit each year.

However, this is not where the connection between Bill Goldfinch and this museum ends. There is another aircraft at Bungay that warrants attention – in the form of a small blue amphibian.

Bill Goldfinch had continued his love of aircraft outside of his service in the RAF and had built a Luton Minor, G-AYDY, in the 1970s, flying it until he sold it in the early 1980s. At the time of writing it is kept flyable in Ireland. However, at his local airfield of Old Sarum in Wiltshire, Bill worked five days a week for eleven years on an amphibian aircraft project, the Amphibian 161. He wanted to design a light two-seat floatplane capable of being built at home with the intention of marketing it through the Popular Flying Association. Very much an ingenious contraption that, true to the prisoner of war spirit, utilised many every-day items for all manner of aeronautical functions. Bill took influence from both the Grumman Duck and numerous Loening amphibious aircraft designs.

Tragically Bill never completed the 161, although his colleague Tony Butler, who had assisted him, was fully aware of his plans for the aircraft. After completing initial taxiing tests at the airfield, the authorities, concerned about the apparent lack of insurance, asked him to conduct further tests at a different location. Bill died on 2 October 2007, the day before the 161 was due to have undertaken its second set of taxiing and water trials.

Upon passing to the care of the museum at Flixton, the 161 was taken under the wing of museum member David Dawson, who with the help of Tony once more, finished the 161 as Bill would have wanted.

ALTENBURG MUSEUM REPLICA
The Lower Attic, Colditz Castle

One of the main attractions in the Lower Attic of Colditz Castle is the full size, non-flying replica of the glider built by the World Flight Altenburg Nobitz Museum. The idea for the build started in 2008 after

Above: Originally housed at the Deutsche Tecknik Museum in Berlin, the Altenburg replica now resides on public display in the Lower Attic at Colditz Castle. (Author)

---

a visit to the castle by the museum's representatives. The team was looking to build a vintage glider for its museum and, inspired by the Colditz Cock, and after acquiring the plans, construction started in September 2009.

The construction was carried out by eight men, all of whom have clearly defined roles. The project leader, Witold Stelzer, oversaw the whole construction programme and interpreted the plans, his background having been as an Aeronautical Engineering Lecturer in the GDR. Dietmar Flache managed primarily the construction of the wings and tail surfaces, whilst Andy Drabek took responsibility for the fuselage. Five other members of the museum carried out the fabrication of other minor parts together with the stitching and covering of the glider. The completed glider was rolled out in April 2011 and, although intended as a static machine only, the glider had been constructed with aviation quality materials and other than some modifications to the control system, is true to the original. An attempt was actually made by the team following completion of the project to fly it by bungee launch. However, after one attempt in which the glider failed to become airborne, all future plans to fly the machine were abandoned.

At that time there was no space at Colditz for the replica glider to be housed there, so in May 2012 it was transported by the Altenburg members to the Deutsche Tecknik Museum in Gatow, Berlin. After the castle's renovations, the glider moved to Colditz in October 2014.

COLDITZ COCK FLYING REPLICA PROTOTYPE
The Glider Heritage Centre, Lasham, Hampshire

The former Second World War airfield at Lasham in Hampshire boasts both the Lasham Gliding Society and, more recently, the Glider Heritage Centre (GHC). The runways that used to reverberate to the noise of Mosquitoes, Typhoons, Hurricanes and Spitfires, now enjoy the somewhat quiet retirement offered by the gliders and club tugs that fly daily.

Above: Our first, test, Colditz Cock replica pictured after having been reassembled in the Glider Heritage Centre at Lasham. (Author)

Above: Our replica hanging from the roof at Lasham. (Paul Haliday)

Opened for the first time to the public in August 2013, with the completion of a large hangar to house historically significant airworthy gliders, it was the ideal location for us to place our first, prototype, Colditz glider. Having had no need to use it in an emergency in Germany, the prototype had sat in my store, located above the spray booth in my workshop, for around a year.

With the imminent opening of the GHC and its desire to gather together the more significant airframes into one place, I approached them to see if they wished to home our replica, which they gracefully did. After clearing the workshop schedule for a week, Pat Willis carried out the necessary repairs to the lower fuselage structure damage caused by our test flights the previous year. With the addition of hard points to the top surface of the wings and tail, our prototype was ready to go to her new home. A small contingent arrived from the museum the following week, and transported the glider to Lasham, Pat and I following a few days later. We assembled the machine in the back of the new museum and within days it was hoisted into the roof with the other

Above: The RAF Escape Association's scale replica at East Kirkby. (Author)

static gliders. It pleases me to know that our little contribution to the story of the men of Colditz will be there for many more years to come.

THE RAF ESCAPE ASSOCIATION SCALE REPLICA
The Lincolnshire Aviation Heritage Centre, East Kirkby, Lincolnshire

Lincolnshire. Bomber country. Modern day home to the Battle of Britain Memorial Flight, but steeped in Bomber Command history at nearly every road sign. Scampton, famous for the Dambuster raids of 1943, Binbrook, Hemswell, Digby, Woodhall Spa, Wickenby, Waddington – the list goes on.

In the north-east of the county, out of sight of the spires of the iconic Lincoln Cathedral, lies East Kirkby, home of the Lincolnshire Aviation Museum. Farming brothers Fred and Harold Panton formed the museum to commemorate the loss of their brother Chris Panton, a Pilot Officer Engineer killed in a 433 Squadron Handley-Page Halifax during a mission to Nuremberg on the night of 30 March 1944. The Panton brothers acquired Lancaster NX611 to act as a memorial to their brother, and after moving it to East Kirkby, they formed a museum around it. Opened in July 1988, the museum now welcomes tens of thousands of visitors a year. The Lancaster now carries out regular 'taxi' runs at the airfield, but the main goal is for her to fly again.

It is obvious that the main draw of the crowds is the Lancaster, but in a small side building, close to the preserved control tower, is housed the RAF Escape Association Collection. The Escape Association was formed as a charitable organisation in 1946 with the aim of helping and assisting those in the Occupied Europe who risked their lives to help downed RAF aircrew escape or evade capture by the Germans. The Association was disbanded in 1995, at which point its archives and artefacts, together with those from a number of other organisations such as the Caterpillar and Goldfish clubs, moved to the Lincolnshire Aviation Museum.

The collection tells the significant story of escape and evasion, the duty of every Allied airman brought down during operations over enemy territory, during the Second World War. It includes many items made or used by PoWs. Hung in the roof of the main room is a substantial 50% scale model of the Colditz Cock which is half covered in gingham fabric, half exposed to show the internal structure. Below it the story of the inmates of Colditz Castle is told, together with newspaper cuttings detailing the exploits of those, like our team, who have endeavoured to test the escape theory over the decades since 1945.

THE MARTIN FRANCIS REPLICA
Derbyshire

Deep in the High Peak of Derbyshire flourishes a project with years of dedication in the making. Martin Francis, a retired engineer with fourteen years' service at British Aerospace, Woodford, has embarked on perhaps the most significant 'Cock' replica to grace the skies of the future. A keen aeromodeller at heart, his interest first came from reading an article in *Flight* magazine in 1968. The desire to build a quarter-scale flying model of the Colditz glider grew, and Martin spent years researching through the available books of the time, as well as contacting former inmates of the Castle. Eventually, the model was

Above: The remarkable Colditz Cock glider being constructed to a very high standard by Martin Francis. (Jeff and Martin Francis)

completed and successfully flown in 1981, its flight characteristics clearly proving the veracity of Bill Goldfinch's design.

Meanwhile, Martin learned to glide with the Avro Gliding Club at Woodford, and his thoughts soon turned to producing a full-size flying 'Cock' replica. At Woodford he became acquainted with Peter Teagle, glider pilot and BGA Senior Inspector, and a young Aeronautical Engineer, Julian Mills. Martin's research continued steadily, and he first visited *Schloss* Colditz in 1985 whilst it was still behind the 'Iron Curtain'. His passion grew, and a start was made on the full-size working drawings. A series of life events, including a near-fatal road accident, held up further development of the replica for some years.

A return to gliding in 1999 reignited Martin's desire to pursue the full-size replica build. Thus, later that year, his project was registered with the British Gliding Association. Initially under the watchful eye of Peter Teagle, the assigned BGA Senior Inspector, and with technical support from Julian Mills, preparations moved ahead, some of which involved alterations to house and garage to accommodate such a machine! Additionally, there was much input by Peter Underwood from the BGA Technical Committee, leading to the acquisition of technical data, stress analysis calculations and proof testing of vital components.

Construction proper began in 2001 and continued apace until, with the wings completed, came Peter Teagle's retirement from active engineering and Reg Wooller became the new Senior Inspector overseeing the project. Also at this time, another former Woodford colleague, Howard Apps, generously offered his aeronautical design expertise which has since proved to be of considerable support. Working as and when life permitted, Martin has continued the build, culminating at the end of the summer of 2015 with the first rig of the glider in a neighbour's garden.

Speaking of his project, Martin commented: 'I'm not working to a time limit or a date. It's a hobby – it'll be ready when it is ready.' Stressed for both aero-towing and winch launching, the project follows as accurately as possible the drawings as plotted by Bill Goldfinch back in 1944. Obviously, deviations have had to be made to satisfy the regulatory authorities and, although most of the metal fittings are of Martin's own design, they are influenced either by gliders of the same period, or from post-war kit-build aircraft such as the Clutton 'Fred' and Luton Minor from which Bill Goldfinch took the inspiration for the rudder of his design.

Clearly the project is nearing completion, but with no set timescale, some minor structure additions, and the covering to be applied, it will be some time yet. However, the prospect of a fully airworthy manned Colditz glider taking to the skies, not for a limited number of flights, but for what will hopefully be a long and successful career, is very exciting. In the months and years to come, the skies above the Peak District will be the place to watch.

References and Notes

Chapter 1: **OFFIZIERSLAGER IV-C, COLDITZ CASTLE**
1. Major P.R. Reid, *The Colditz Story* (Coronet Books, London, 1972), p.103.
2. Reinhold Eggers, *Colditz, The German Viewpoint* (NEL, London, 1974), p.41.
3. Airey Neave, *They Have their Exits* (Coronet Books, London, 1973), pp.79-92.
4. Henry Chancellor, *Colditz, The Definitive History* (Coronet Books, London, 2002), p.175.
5. Whilst Rothenberger's nickname is generally spelt as 'Franz Joseph' (see for example, Michael Booker, *Collecting Colditz and Its Secrets*, Grub Street, London, 2005), the Emperor's name is also spelt Franz Josef.
6. Henry Chancellor, *ibid*, pp.221-30.
7. Georg Martin Schaedlich, *Tales From Colditz Castle* (Thomas Schaedlilch, Colditz, 2003), p.75.
8. Reinhold Eggers, *Colditz, The German Viewpoint* (New English Library, 1961), pp.150-2.
9. Anon, *Colditz: A Pictorial History* (Caxton Editions, London, 2001), p.122.
10. Reinhold Eggers, *ibid*, p.152.

Chapter 2: **THE COLDITZ COCK**
1. Obituary in *The Daily Telegraph*, 12 October 2007.
2. Interview with Jack Best, courtesy of the Colditz Society.
3. Henry Chancellor, *op.cit.*, pp.335-6.
4. Obituary in *The Daily Telegraph*, 8 February 2008. This states that 'It was Rolt who was the first inmate of Colditz to propose building a glider, although Flight Lieutenant Bill Goldfinch revealed that he had been thinking along the same lines'.
5. ibid.
6. Jack Champ and Colin Burgess, *The Diggers of Colditz* (Orbis, London, 1985), p.195.
7. Andy Russell, 'The Colditz Glider - The First Idea', in the *Colditz Appreciation Society Newsletter*, September 2007.
8. Jim Rogers, *Tunnelling into Colditz, A Mining Engineer in Captivity* (Robert Hale, London, 1986), p.189.
9. Chancellor, *op.cit.*, p.341.
10. Interview with Bill Goldfinch, courtesy of the Colditz Society.
11. P.R. Reid, *The Latter Days at Colditz* (Cassell, London, 2003), pp.279-89.
12. Champ and Burgess, *op. cit.*, p.195.

13. Dianne Rutherford, 'The Liberation of Colditz Castle', quoted on the Australian War Memorial's website: www.awm.gov.au

14. C.H. Latimer-Needham, 'The Colditz Cock', *Flight International*, 26 September 1968.

Chapter 3: **THE CHALLENGE**

1. In 1954, the Luftfahrt-Bundesamt (LBA) was founded to assist the West German Federal Ministry of Transport. At the same time, Dr. Ing. Hans-Christoph Seebohm, the then Federal Minister of Transport and former President of the Chamber of Industry and Commerce in Braunschweig, nominated the city of Braunschweig to be the seat of the Office of Civil Aviation. One argument which he put forward in favour of Braunschweig and which showed his far-sightedness was the central location of the Authority in a re-united Germany. Initially with a staff of just twenty-eight, the LBA officially began its work on 1 February 1955.

2. The subsequent television programme, *Dambusters: Building The Bouncing Bomb*, was awarded a Royal Television Society award for best history programme in March 2012.

Chapter 4: **THE BUILD BEGINS**

1. Maunfactured by Alexander Schleicher GmbH & Co, ironically not that far from Colditz, the ASK 21 is a glass-reinforced plastic two-seater mid-wing glider aircraft with a T-tail. The ASK 21 is designed primarily for beginner instruction, but is also suitable for cross-country flying and aerobatic instruction.

Chapter 5: **COLDITZ HERE WE COME**

1. In recent years part of the German quarters within Colditz Castle has been converted into a youth hostel, offering visitors the opportunity to stay at this legendary Second World War site – albeit in better surroundings than enjoyed by the PoWs. For more information visit: www.jugendherberge.de

Chapter 6: **READY TO ROLL**

1. The only known photograph of the original Colditz glider was taken in the middle of April 1945 by Lee Carson, one of two American newspaper correspondents assigned to the task force which liberated the castle. The date when the image was taken is variously given as the 15th or the 17th of the month. Writing in the September 2007 issue of the *Colditz Appreciation Society Newsletter*, Andy Russell notes that 'the photo of the glider was … traced to California by Mr. Walter L. Leschander who having read Pat Reid's book, then searched all America to find it. This is the only proof of its one time existence and many would not believe its story until they saw this photo. On the rear of the picture is the hand script date April 17th, 1945, the day before evacuation began and prisoners returned to their homeland.' Lee Carson attended Smith College, Chicago, aged 14, and left, aged 16, to become a reporter for the *Chicago Times*. In 1940 she joined the International News Service, being made a War Correspondent in 1943. Carson was dubbed by her colleagues as 'the best looking' female War Correspondent – and reportedly used this to her advantage.